WITTGENSTEIN STUDIES

THOEMMES

Printed in Great Britain
by Antony Rowe Ltd

WITTGENSTEIN STUDIES

A Study in
Wittgenstein's *Tractatus*

ALEXANDER MASLOW

THOEMMES PRESS

This edition published by Thoemmes Press, 1997

Thoemmes Press
11 Great George Street
Bristol BS1 5RR, England

US office: Distribution and Marketing
22883 Quicksilver Drive
Dulles, Virginia 20166, USA

ISBN 1 85506 538 X

This is a reprint of the 1961 edition

Publisher's Note

The publisher has gone to great lengths to ensure the
quality of this reprint but points out that some
imperfections in the original book may be apparent.

TO THE MEMORY OF Moritz Schlick

ERRATA

Page ix, line 8 from bottom, *for* My book *read* The
          book
Page 43, line 8, *for* last chapter *read* third chapter
Page 114, line 7 from bottom, *for* published in 1918
          read published in 1919
Page 124, line 6 from bottom, *for* p. 121 *read* p. 99

MASLOW: A STUDY IN WITTGENSTEIN'S TRACTATUS
MARCH, 1961

Preface

This study in Wittgenstein's *Tractatus* is substantially as it was written in 1933. By the time I had finished my study, the importance of the *Tractatus* in philosophical circles was on the wane, probably because of Wittgenstein's deprecating attitude toward his own book. But the recent revival of interest in the *Tractatus* leads me now to think that the essay may be of interest to contemporary philosophers, and so I have decided to publish it.

Strangely, no book in English dealt exclusively with the *Tractatus* until 1959, when Miss G. E. M. Anscombe brought out her *Introduction to Wittgenstein's Tractatus,* largely concerned with logical details of the *Tractatus* and especially valuable, I think, because it shows the essential connections of Wittgenstein with Frege, Russell, and Ramsey. Another book, *Wittgenstein's Tractatus,* by E. Stenius, has lately been announced for publication, and there are rumors of still others on the way. It is unfortunate that Friedrich Waismann, who was so close to Wittgenstein shortly after the *Tractatus* was finished, has not published his book, though it was announced about thirty years ago.

My study was written very largely from the point of view of logical positivism, a view I no longer hold. Quite appropriately, as it seems to me now, my struggles with the obscurities of the *Tractatus* gradually forced me to reconsider many of my own philosophical convictions (some of which, previously, I had not even been aware of), and by the time I had finished writing my essay, I had pretty well finished with my positivism as well. I climbed through it, over it, and threw away the ladder. As a consequence I no longer agree with everything I wrote in this study, especially with some of my criticisms of Wittgenstein. I thought that he was often backsliding into metaphysics, which is, of course, a mortal sin for a positivist. Taking into account this change in my philosophical outlook, I am inclined to think that a thorough revision of my essay is inadvisable. However, these present disagreements that I have with my former views do not extend to the essentials of my interpretation of the *Tractatus,* which I still consider to be sound. Hence, I have decided to let the study stand, save for a very few changes, practically as it was written in 1933.

I am grateful to the publishing house of Routledge and Kegan Paul for permission to quote from the 1922 edition of Wittgenstein's *Tractatus Logico-Philosophicus,* and to the University of California Press for painstaking editing of my manuscript.

Finally, I thank my wife for her long and unfailing patience in correcting the vagaries of my English.

ALEXANDER MASLOW

University of British Columbia, Vancouver
August, 1959

Introduction

It was with hesitation that I undertook an exposition of Ludwig Wittgenstein's *Tractatus Logico-Philosophicus,* and, after two years of effort, I find with a grim satisfaction that my presentiments are well substantiated. The *Tractatus* still remains for me in some details a closed book; and, while I have a more or less definite opinion of the fundamentals of Wittgenstein's view, I do not feel confident enough to assert that my interpretation of the *Tractatus* does represent accurately and faithfully Wittgenstein's own point of view. I do feel, however, that in essentials I have caught the spirit of the book.

The most formidable obstacle to understanding the *Tractatus* lies, as can be seen even from its first few sentences, in the obscure style of Wittgenstein's presentation. Although the *Tractatus* has a peculiar poetic charm, its terse, cryptic, aphoristic pronouncements are not conducive to clear understanding. My book might well serve as an outline of Wittgenstein's view for those who have already been initiated into it, but it can hardly be considered as a satisfactory exposition for the novice. Wittgenstein's own statement in his Preface, that 'This book will perhaps only be understood by those who have themselves already thought the thoughts which are expressed in it', although probably intended to refer to the intrinsic difficulties of the subject, is really a good, even

if not intended, comment on its style. The difficulty in understanding the *Tractatus* probably lies deeper than merely its
style of presentation. It may be due to an unresolved philosophical conflict in Wittgenstein at the time he was jotting
down his ideas during his service with the Austrian Army
in World War I. On the flyleaf of Moritz Schlick's copy of
the *Tractatus* Wittgenstein wrote, 'Jeder dieser Sätze ist der
Ausdruck einer Krankheit' ('Every one of these propositions is the expression of an illness'). My guess is that this
Krankheit was due, at least on the philosophic level, to the
conflict between Wittgenstein's growing positivistic convictions and his metaphysical tendencies. In the background of
his pithy pronouncements one hears not only the clear voices
of Frege and Russell but the muffled voices of Kant, Schopenhauer, Plato, and even St. Augustine. And this conflict is
reflected even in Wittgenstein's vocabulary.

But whatever the explanation, the fact remains that the
Tractatus is in many of its passages so obscure that it would be
impossible, I believe, to gather the fundamentals of Wittgenstein's view without some help from people who have been
initiated into it directly by the author himself. Unfortunately,
not much has been written on Wittgenstein by people well
acquainted with him. My main sources of information here
were Bertrand Russell, F. P. Ramsey, and Moritz Schlick.

Among the philosophical writings I used in connection
with this essay, Russell's works naturally play a predominant
part. Wittgenstein was a pupil of Russell's, and Russell's
influence on Wittgenstein, we may conclude, must have been
very great; externally this is substantiated by the fact that
Russell is alluded to in the *Tractatus* (unfortunately mostly
without specific references) more often than anyone else. In
fact, except for a few references to Frege, Russell's is the
only name that appears in the *Tractatus* with any frequency.
The obvious dependence on Russell did not, however, prevent
Wittgenstein from severely criticizing his teacher, as will be

seen in my third chapter. Since Russell has influenced me more than any other contemporary philosopher, my interpretation of the *Tractatus* has probably been more affected by Russell than I am consciously aware of, though I frequently disagree with him. F. P. Ramsey's writings were of help in clearing up some details of the *Tractatus*. Many details of my exposition of the *Tractatus* are derived from the lectures of and discussions with Professor Schlick, and I have been generally strongly influenced by Schlick's logical positivism or, as he himself prefers to call it, consistent empiricism. Yet I differ considerably from Schlick in my basic interpretation of the philosophy underlying the *Tractatus*. I believe that the *Tractatus* is much more metaphysical than Schlick considers it to be.

In current philosophic literature references to Wittgenstein are frequent but incidental. The only articles so far [1933] published in English on Wittgenstein which are worth mentioning in this connection are: Professor Schlick's article in the *Proceedings of the Seventh International Congress of Philosophy*, and his articles in the *College of the Pacific Publications in Philosophy;* and 'Logical Positivism' by A. E. Blumberg and H. Feigl in the *Journal of Philosophy,* May 21, 1931. Wittgenstein himself since the appearance of the *Tractatus* has published only one short article, 'Some Remarks on Logical Form', in the *Aristotelian Society Supplementary Volume IX*, 1929. The promised book on Wittgenstein by Friedrich Waismann is long overdue.

Though I have used Russell, Ramsey, and Schlick extensively, I do not attempt to draw explicit connections between their views and those of Wittgenstein, except occasionally in the case of Russell. Since my purpose in writing this book is merely to make a sensible and, so far as I can, consistent interpretation of the *Tractatus,* I have adopted Wittgenstein's attitude: 'How far my efforts agree with those of other philosophers I will not decide. Indeed what I have here written makes no claim to novelty in points of detail; and therefore I give no sources, because it is indifferent to me whether what I have thought has already been thought before me by another' (*Tractatus*, Preface). It would, of course, be possible to show some parallels and many contrasts between the views of Wittgenstein and those of many other philosophers, but I have usually avoided doing this. Whenever I quote from or refer to other philosophers I do so merely as a device of exposition, namely, to bring out some vague feature of the topic under discussion by appealing to the familiar views of well-known philosophers. I do not intend to impute to Wittgenstein the views of the authors quoted, but I use the quotations merely as rhetorical illuminations unless, of course, I have otherwise indicated. My main purpose here is to understand Wittgenstein, and I find that to be a sufficiently difficult task without lengthy comparisons with other philosophers.

I am making a rather free interpretation of the *Tractatus,* and I do not attempt to separate sharply the strictly expository part of my work from the interpretational and even the commentatorial. I am merely trying to make intelligible what I feel to be important in the views embodied in the *Tractatus*. I do not always follow the order of the *Tractatus* or give the same relative weight to the topics as in Wittgenstein's own presentation. Some important topics of the book I merely touch upon, and I have almost entirely omitted some of the most important topics, such as the foundations of mathematics. The *Tractatus* is so condensed that to give an adequate treatment to all the subjects it deals with would require volumes, and more thorough acquaintance with Wittgenstein's view than I can claim. On the whole what I try to do in my book is this: Out of the enigmatic text I have attempted to construct a reasonable account of the philosophical essentials of Wittgenstein's view in the *Tractatus;* in places I criticize and even reject some details of his view as I understand it.

It is, of course, quite likely that in my criticism I am often fighting a straw man, and that my final interpretation would not suit the author of the *Tractatus*.

The obscure style of the *Tractatus* opens possibilities for numerous interpretations. In the original process of trying to understand the *Tractatus*, I made several starts but found none of them entirely satisfactory. Sooner or later a chosen line of approach led into what seemed to be a blind alley, and I had to start anew. My final choice is not entirely satisfactory, for it leaves some parts of the book still unintelligible or self-contradictory. But the view I present in this essay is the best of the alternatives I have been able to find so far. I feel that finding the right initial approach to the *Tractatus* is the most important and difficult task of my whole enterprise. It cannot be attained merely by an orderly process of analyzing the book in detail, but must be arrived at by something like an intuitive grasp of the underlying motive of the author. I feel that, if one could only, to use a metaphor, strike the right key from the beginning and give the proper meanings to Wittgenstein's essential terms, such as atomic fact, object, and form, one could go on without much trouble into the rest of this syncopated philosophical composition. To use another metaphor (Wittgenstein himself was very fond of metaphors), the *Tractatus* at first approach is like a picture puzzle, which presents the problem of finding the point of view from which hidden figures can be seen in the chaotic conglomeration of shapes and colors. Perhaps by my efforts at solving the puzzle I have discovered figures not intended by the author himself! But metaphors apart, after several trials, and taking the cue from Russell's Introduction to the *Tractatus*, I have chosen to interpret the book as an inquiry into the formal aspects of the means of knowledge, that is, into language or symbolism in general. But I have expanded the meaning and scope of language as universal symbolism so that in my interpretation of the *Tractatus* the basic phi-

losophy underlying it has become a kind of Kantian phenomenalism, with the forms of language playing a role similar
to Kant's transcendental apparatus. Language in this interpretation is not only an instrument of thought and communication but also an all-pervading factor in organizing our
cognitive experience. Here my interpretation goes beyond the
limits of logical positivism, even though generally in dealing
with the *Tractatus* I have tried to keep as much as possible
within the logico-positivistic frame. The essentials of my
consequent understanding of the philosophy of Wittgenstein
are as follows.

Language is the activity in which we use some parts of our
experience—spoken words, written words, images, and so on
—to represent other parts of it and to connect them into a
system of interrelating facts within the world in such a way
that certain facts used as symbols express certain other facts.
Until so interpreted and interrelated, our experience is chaotic
and is not an organized world. Thus, we cannot actually
separate organized and communicable experience of our world
from the language by means of which we know it; and we
can discuss the language separately only in abstraction. Language and thought are inseparable, and an investigation of
the formal structure of language thus becomes thought's self-
clarification.

Philosophy is not merely a passive love of wisdom but,
more importantly, the active search for it. Its aim is a part
of our aim to understand the world; but in our striving toward
that end philosophy plays a special role: it clarifies our
thought or language, which necessarily precedes the activity
of ascertaining the truth or falsity of our thought. Philosophy
itself is not concerned with the empirical finding of the truths
about the world; that is the business of everyday practical
activity and of its refined extension, science. Neither does
philosophy consist of sets or systems of propositions about
the world already established as true. The peculiar contri-

bution of philosophy to our wisdom lies in the activity of the formal clarification of our thought or language. The separation of the functions of scientist and philosopher is theoretically clear and complete, though in actual life it is not hard and fast because the two functions are often performed by the same person, and are two aspects of one and the same search for wisdom. The philosopher looks for clarity and validity of thought, the scientist for its truth, but, since both these activities tend to relieve the feeling of intellectual discomfort, even if in different ways, the result is that very often the two functions are not only actually fused in the same person but also become confused. Traditional philosophy is, according to Wittgenstein, full of this confusion, and the *Tractatus* is essentially a philosophical discussion of the formal prerequisites of all valid thought, that is, of all symbolism, designed to eliminate this confusion.

The main thesis of the *Tractatus* is summarized in the profound triviality: 'What can be said at all can be said clearly; and whereof one cannot speak thereof one must be silent'. In other words, in any discussion worthy of the name we must confine ourselves to talking sense. The *Tractatus* itself is largely an attempt to analyze the formal aspects of the medium of making sense, that is, of language or symbolism in general, and to show what is essential to any symbolism in order that it be significant and not merely a series of noises and marks. More precisely, the main problem of the *Tractatus* is to show the necessary prerequisites of an ideal symbolism, to which all our actual languages must conform as far as practically possible in order to serve their fundamental purpose of being a medium of knowledge. With the aesthetic and affective aspects of symbolism Wittgenstein is not concerned. Neither does he investigate empirically the existent natural languages; philological study is far from his purpose. He restricts his investigation to the formal or logical prerequisites of any possible language, of all possible symbolisms.

The discussion of the formal or logical prerequisites of all
symbolism is not intended to be taken as saying anything
about the actual state of affairs in the world: 'What lies in
its application logic cannot anticipate' (5.557). Of course,
all our knowledge about the world comes through the medium
of language, and therefore the formal structure of the world
(the world we know—we cannot talk about any other) is
inseparable from the language we use: *The limits of my
language* mean the limits of my world' (5.6). But formal
aspects of language do not determine anything about the
actual content of the world; we cannot infer existence from
logic. The formal prerequisites of our language and therefore
of the world would be just as valid if the state of affairs in
the world were different from what it actually is, or even if
there were no world at all: 'Everything we can describe at
all could also be otherwise' (5.634). That the world, if there
be any world, must be such that we could think about it is
merely a tautology and gives us no more information about
the actual state of affairs than such a pseudo-proposition
as '*A* is *A*'.

Strictly speaking, the formal prerequisites of our language
or thought cannot even be discussed. They permeate all our
language, and in order to *say* something factual *about* them,
we would have to put ourselves outside language, that is, to
say something while remaining silent, which is an impossibility. The final clarification of our thought, the realization
of its formal conditions, is a matter for philosophic activity
and not for significant propositions. The discussion of the
Tractatus is, then, but a verbal elucidation, an attempt to
bring the reader to the realization of what he himself already
knows, of that 'which cannot be said', but which nevertheless,
is essential to all significant saying, and which 'shows itself'
in every discourse. This is our logocentric predicament, and
on Wittgenstein's view it includes the egocentric as well.

Besides discussing the formal prerequisites of language

and the limits of cognition as determined by these prerequisites, the *Tractatus* also comes to a positive conclusion of great moment, namely, that our life experience is, after all, not limited to the sphere of symbolic cognition. Our cognition cannot exhaust reality, and outside the knowable there is also the realm of the *mystical,* which cannot be a subject of any discourse. Any attempt to discuss the mystical leads to talking nonsense; and many traditional philosophers make the serious error of attempting to discuss this undiscussable in their pretension of talking from an angelic point of view.

The chapters of my book do not follow the divisions of the *Tractatus.* Roughly, my first chapter corresponds in essentials to the first and the second chapters of the *Tractatus;* my second chapter deals primarily with the third chapter of the *Tractatus;* my third chapter deals with some of the more technical aspects of Wittgenstein's view in Chaps. 4, 5, and 6 of the *Tractatus;* and my last chapter is a presentation of his views on philosophy. Although I group my chapters around some fundamental notions of the chapters of the *Tractatus,* in my discussion of these topics I do not limit myself to the material offered in only the corresponding chapters of the *Tractatus,* but draw my information freely from any part of the book I find useful for the purpose at hand. I usually indicate this by special references in parentheses to the numbered paragraphs of the *Tractatus.* Most of my original contributions are in the first two chapters of my book.

My first chapter is grouped around the fundamental notions of object and atomic fact. Here I discuss primarily the general principles underlying Wittgenstein's view on language or symbolism.

My second chapter is primarily a continuation of the discussion of the first chapter on language, but it is narrowed down to more specific topics, namely, the nature of symbol and sign. In order to elucidate the important opening paragraphs of the third chapter of the *Tractatus,* I insert at the beginning of my second chapter a short discussion on thought and logic.

The central theme of my third chapter is Wittgenstein's view of molecular propositions as truth functions of atomic propositions, and around this I group the kindred topics of logical propositions and inference. I close the chapter with a discussion of Whitehead and Russell's *Principia Mathematica* in the light of Wittgenstein's view on logic. This chapter is the least original part of my study. A reader not interested in logical technicalities can omit this chapter without missing the basic ideas of my interpretation of Wittgenstein.

In my fourth and last chapter I present Wittgenstein's view of the nature and role of philosophy, and I give some space to his solipsism and mysticism. Wittgenstein's solipsism throws light on his central theme, the role of language. His mysticism supplements his positivism, and thus provides for experiences outside the limits imposed by language.

My grasp of the subject is not sufficiently secure to allow as yet of a crystallized vocabulary. My occasional vagueness in language reflects the uncertainty and amorphousness of my view at present; and thus, the very shortcomings in my essay seem to substantiate, in a rather negative fashion, the view defended here that thought and language are inseparable. I am also aware of a certain choppiness in my presentation of the subject. Slightly paraphrasing Bradley, I might say that if I saw clearer I should be shorter and more orderly and precise in my presentation. I can express my feelings here in no better way than by quoting verbatim another remark of Bradley's: 'It means that on all questions, if you push me far enough, at present I end in doubts and perplexities'.

My attempt at presenting Wittgenstein's view does not pretend, I repeat, to be either complete or entirely correct. I can only hope that it is in accord with the essentials of Wittgenstein's original view at least in spirit, and that my criticisms of the *Tractatus* are in the direction of Wittgenstein's

own changes after he wrote the book. In spite of Wittgenstein's later neglect and even disparagement of the *Tractatus,*
I still believe it to be a great book, and my hope is that this
essay will make a contribution to the understanding of the
man who has been considered by many of his very competent
peers to be one of the greatest contemporary philosophers.

A. M.

University of California, Berkeley
December, 1933

Contents

3   Truth Functions of Atomic Propositions   95

4   Wittgenstein's Philosophy   137

Absorption in the study of the supernatural is most harmful.
CONFUCIUS

Objects, Atomic Facts, and Language

This chapter is primarily concerned with what I consider to be the most important idea underlying the *Tractatus*—the pervading role of language in all our cognitive experience—and with the closely related ideas of object and atomic fact.

1.1 Wittgenstein's purpose in the *Tractatus* is to investigate the formal requirements of all correct symbolism or language in broad sense, and thus of all possible knowledge. Language, in this wide sense of the term, is the activity in which we use systematically some parts of our experience to represent according to some rules certain other parts; in this way we can interrelate our experience and thus construct a world. Until so interpreted the sheer data of our experience would not constitute any world, would be meaningless, and we could not even speak of it. Thus the relation between our language or thought on one hand and the world we know (and there is only one world for us, the one that we do know) on the other is so intimate that we cannot actually separate the two, and can discuss them separately only in abstraction. The relation between language and the world is, in Wittgenstein's terminology, internal: we cannot separate the world from the perspective of the language by means of which we organize it. As Wittgenstein expresses this, '*The limits of my language* mean the limits of my world' (5.6),[1] and 'The facts in logical space are the world' (1.13), where by the 'logical space' is meant the formal or grammatical requirements of language we use. Thus, on this view an investigation of the formal aspects of language is at the same time an investigation of the formal aspects of our world: 'To give the essence of propositions means to give the essence of all description, therefore the essence of the world' (5.4711).

The first and second chapters of the *Tractatus* give a summary survey of the formal characteristics of the possible world. On my interpretation, no metaphysical discussion of the ultimate stuff of the world is intended here; any such discussion should be considered, on Wittgenstein's view, as nonsense. The discussion starts from and is limited by the language we actually use at the time of our philosophizing about the world. To attempt to get beyond the world of *our* experience to the 'real' world in itself would require us to take an 'angelic' point of view, to jump out of our intellectual skins, so to speak, and would be a plain self-contradiction. Sentences torn from their context in *our* experience, not interpreted from *our* perspective, are neither true nor false to us, but are for us simply nonsensical; and a proposition from an angelic point of view would be a nonsensical sentence for us —we do not happen to be angels. In refusing to make nonsensical statements about the world 'in itself', we really do not make any assertions or denials about the nature of that world; we merely point out the logical restrictions to which any discourse is to be limited if it is to be a sensible discourse and not nonsensical sound- or mark-making. We are merely drawing attention here to the tautological requirement for any sensible language: we can give sense to our propositions only within *our* experience and therefore according to the rules

---

[1] Numbers in parentheses refer to the numbered sections of the first edition of the *Tractatus*.

of *our* language. Thus the discussion of the formal characteristics of the world, of *our* world, is nonmetaphysical.

I shall return again and again to this topic of the relation between language in a wide sense of the term and the world, but now I will pass to a somewhat more detailed exposition of the *Tractatus*.

The formal requirement made upon the world in the first chapter of the *Tractatus* is that the world, if there be a world, must consist of facts: 'The world is the totality of facts, not of things' (1.1), and 'The world divides into facts' (1.2). The very term 'world' in our language implies complexity, that is, facts. It is impossible to have a world until we interrelate the noncomplex or simple elements of our experience into complexes or facts. Of course, we need not assume here any specific character for these facts or complexes, but we must admit the general requirement of complexity in the world.

The actual and specific character of the facts in the world is found empirically and cannot be derived from an a priori discourse, as rationalists would have it: 'There is no order of things a priori' (5.634). That there *is* a world is an empirical fact, and 'Everything we see could also be otherwise' (5.634). Logically there need be no world at all, but, if there be one, it must comply with this minimum formal requirement, namely, it must be complex, that is, must consist of facts. A world cannot be merely one simple entity, or merely an aggregate of entirely isolated simple entities. A bare 'being' of one simple entity by itself is meaningless. The very modicum of meaning requires another entity of some kind which can be used as a sign of the meaning of the first entity; and this sign has to be interpreted, put into a 'perspective' or context of language, which leads to still further interconnection of entities, namely, to facts. The minimum formal requirement even for naming a simple entity is a fact made up of three entities: *A* is in some relation to *B* for *C*. If the world were not complex, then, as Parmenides said, 'it is neither named, nor expressed, nor opined, nor known, nor perceived by anyone' (Plato, *Parmenides,* 142A).

But, furthermore, even if we managed to name the isolated simple entities within our experience, that would not be sufficient to give us the world, but would be merely an inventory of its simple elements. If our experience could not be grouped into complexes or facts, we could make no propositions, true or false, and therefore we could have no discourse, no knowledge, and, finally, no world to discourse about! First, because to express a proposition, even false, we need a complex sign, that is, a fact, as we shall see more in detail in my Chap. 2. And, second, if we are to have the world, some of our propositions must be true. And that means that there must be some facts in the world, namely, the facts represented by the true propositions. This, of course, logically need not be the case, because there is no necessity for any proposition to be true, or even of there being any proposition at all. But then our present discourse would be of no consequence and our world illusory or Fichtean—a possible but fantastic alternative. Without facts we could have no discourse whatsoever, and with one fact alone we could have no world. Thus, if there be a real world, it must consist of facts. 'The world divides into facts' (1.2), and among the facts the fundamental ones are what Wittgenstein calls *atomic facts.* Atomic facts are the facts which have no parts which are facts; and all other facts, that is, molecular facts, are made up of atomic facts. The elements or constituents of atomic facts are called by Wittgenstein *objects.*

The parts of the *Tractatus* dealing with *atomic facts* and *objects* are among the most obscure of the whole book, but I feel that if we could get only a fair understanding of these two terms, we would get close to the very heart of the book. I shall therefore make an attempt to make as clear as possible the meanings of these two terms as I interpret them. My analysis of the *Tractatus* will depend to a large extent on the meanings I give to these terms. The two terms are intimately connected, as can be seen from the statement that 'An atomic fact is a combination of objects' (2.01); if we could get a clear notion of one, the other would become clear as well. My conclusion in this connection, unfortunately, is that I suspect that Wittgenstein, when he wrote the *Tractatus,* was himself rather vague about the intended meanings of these terms, and that therefore it is impossible to make entirely clear what their meanings should be in the *Tractatus.* Before the detailed discussion of these two terms, I shall give a sketch of what I consider to be the fundamental and correct ideas underlying Wittgenstein's presentation of the subject in the *Tractatus.*

One of the logical requirements of any language is that its terms must have unique and unambiguous meanings assigned to them within our experience. This requirement is met by explicit or implicit definitions, and ultimately by what W. E. Johnson calls the 'ostensive definition', that is, by direct pointing to the objects within the accepted context of the discourse in '*the* language which only I understand' (5.62). The objects or *referends*[2] (the term is due to Miss L. S. Stebbing) of our terms are thus established operationally within the context of the accepted specific universe of discourse. These terms are thus relative to our actual use of language, and it is senseless to look for some absolute or ultimate nature of the objects, as well as for the definition of the ultimate nature 'in itself' of the context in which they occur.

But terms alone, even if meaningful, are not sufficient to make a significant universe of discourse; the terms alone do not make a language, just as an aggregate of objects does not make up a world. Terms merely denote their objects, but language must be also capable of expression. Language is not merely a set of signals for known objects and known groups of the objects, but it also must enable us to express all

---

[2] 'Referend' is equivalent to the now commonly used 'designatum' and 'nominatum', ugly terms I do not like [author's note, 1960].

the possible new combinations of objects, that is, possible new states of affairs or facts. Language must not be merely denotative but must also be expressive; it must not only have terms which are meaningful in our experience but it must also be capable of constructing propositions expressing new facts by means of the old terms. The smallest units of expressive language—of any language—are propositions.

Among all the possible propositions of language there must be some simple propositions, that is, propositions not containing any other propositions as constituents, but consisting only of terms in certain relations; all other propositions are constructs out of the simple propositions. The simple propositions we may call *atomic,* and the propositions constructed out of the atomic propositions we may call *molecular:* 'It is obvious that in the analysis of propositions we must come to elementary [atomic] propositions, which consist of names in immediate combination' (4.221).[3]

Knowledge of all the true atomic propositions is theoretically necessary and sufficient for the complete knowledge of the world: 'the introduction of the elementary [atomic] propositions is fundamental for the comprehension of the other kinds of propositions' (4.411), and 'The specification of all true elementary propositions describes the world completely' (4.26). But what makes the true atomic propositions true are the atomic facts.

---

[3] Wittgenstein in the *Tractatus* uses the terms 'elementary proposition' instead of 'atomic proposition', but I am going to use the term 'atomic proposition' by analogy with Wittgenstein's use of the term 'atomic fact'. This is Russell's usage in *The Philosophy of Logical Atomism* and in the second edition of Whitehead and Russell's *Principia Mathematica* and seems to be the general accepted usage nowadays, to which Wittgenstein himself conformed in his article 'Some Remarks on Logical Form', *Aristotelian Society Supplementary,* Vol. IX, 1929, written after the publication of the *Tractatus.* The term 'elementary proposition' is used in the *Principia* in the sense of 'atomic propositions together with all that can be generated from them by means of the stroke applied any finite number of times' (*Principia,* 2d ed., p. xvii). That is, in the *Principia* elementary propositions include molecular propositions but exclude general propositions.

Thus, the actual world we can know (and there is no sense in discoursing about any other) must consist of objects and atomic facts, corresponding respectively to the meaningful terms and the true atomic propositions of *our* universe of discourse. The world is the universe of reference of our significant discourse.

This short sketch represents, I believe, the essentials of what I consider to be clear and sound in Wittgenstein's view on the 'objects' and the 'atomic facts'. I shall proceed with a closer analysis and criticism of these two terms as presented in the *Tractatus,* and especially in the first two chapters of it.

1.2 Atomic fact is defined formally as 'a combination of objects (entities, things)' (2.01); that is, it is a fact which is not in its turn composed of other facts but is a combination of objects. 'Even if the world is infinitely complex, so that every fact consists of an infinite number of atomic facts and every atomic fact is composed of an infinite number of objects, even then there must be objects and atomic facts' (4.2211). Thus objects are what we must find at the end of analysis of facts, and atomic facts are the simplest kind of combination of these last elements of our analysis. This view depends upon what is to be taken as the limit of analysis, and, unfortunately, it is not at all clear from the *Tractatus* what Wittgenstein means by analysis in this connection. What does it mean to say that a fact must be analyzable into atomic facts if this fact has not actually been so analyzed? Can we speak of hidden or unknown atomic facts and objects? And if we engage in the actual analysis, what is the criterion of simplicity and complexity according to which we are to decide in each case whether and when the analysis has come to its ultimate end?

It seems to me that Wittgenstein here is trying to do two things at once without clearly separating them. First, he seems to be making an attempt to give a sketchy account of the actual constitution of our world; at times his account degenerates into metaphysics. Second, Wittgenstein tries to discuss on a nonempirical level the formal requirements of any significant language, of all symbolism, and thus of all possible knowledge, entirely apart from any actual application of these requirements; he does not intend to give here any specific information about the facts in the world but wishes merely to state the universal features of any possible knowledge of the world, or what he calls the logical grammar or logical syntax. Wittgenstein's primary concern, I think, is with the second problem, and the confusion often arises from his digressions into the first; and this confusion of the two problems leads to the initial difficulty in understanding the whole *Tractatus*. Of course (and this is one of the cardinal points of Wittgenstein's view, which I shall return to again), there is no actual separation between language and the world known through its medium; but the two above problems are, nevertheless, theoretically distinct, and we can discuss the problem of the formal requirements of language without factual investigation of the actual world.

1.21   Although the first problem is, on my interpretation of the *Tractatus,* only an irrelevant digression from the proper task of the book, I shall investigate it briefly, to show that Wittgenstein is not at all clear as to what he means by objects and atomic facts. First, however, it is necessary to make a few remarks of a linguistic nature, which would more properly belong to the discussion of the second problem but are indispensable as preliminaries to the discussion of the first. The term 'object' is a variable pseudo-concept (4.1272); it is not a general term formed by a process of abstraction from the perceptual data; it is neither a general name like 'table' or 'red', nor a proper name for an individual in the world. There are no entities in the world for which the term 'object' stands as a proper or general name. 'Object' does not indicate anything in the world, but is a linguistic device for speaking about genuine or generic concepts like 'table' or 'red', or proper names, which when in use do stand for something in reality. 'Object' is a variable standing in an incomplete expression; it is but a blank in a propositional schema or propositional function which is to be filled before this schema acquires definite sense, becomes a significant proposition. It is, for example, the 'x' of $f(x)$. The nature of the 'f' determines the kind of entities whose names or descriptions can serve as the arguments in $f(x)$. Thus 'x is red' is a propositional function which requires that the arguments admissible here must be names or descriptions of spatial entities; 'x' here is merely a device for keeping open the place in the propositional function into which we are to insert a name or a description. Similarly with 'This book is x', where the 'x' stands for a suitable adjective; the suitability is again determined by the nature of the function. Thus the term 'object' does not stand for anything definite in the world, and it would not even appear in a perfect symbolism. But it may be of interest to investigate a little what sort of entities Wittgenstein may have had in mind when he used this term in the *Tractatus*. I have counted at least a dozen kinds of entities which may be suggested by reading the *Tractatus;* among these the three following seem to be of particular interest: sense data, things, and the ontological entities.

1.211   Thus Wittgenstein might have had in mind the sense data when he spoke of objects. He speaks of 'a speck in a visual field . . . *a* tone . . . *a* hardness, etc.' (2.0131). This interpretation would be, probably, most in accord with the general trend of Wittgenstein's view. Objects then would coincide with Hume's *impressions,* if we take into account Hume's own warning that 'By the term impression I would not be understood to express the manner in which our lively perceptions are produced in the soul, *but merely the perceptions themselves;* for which there is no particular name either in the English or any other language, that I know of'.[4] That

---

[4] Footnote on p. 2 of Hume's *Treatise,* Selby-Bigge edition; italics mine.

is, in accord with the positivistic interpretation of Hume. This would also come close to the view of E. Mach, as expressed in his book *The Analysis of Sensations,*[5] as follows:

> The complexes are disintegrated into elements, that is to say, into their ultimate component parts which hitherto we have been unable to subdivide any further . . . Usually, these elements are called sensations. But as vestiges of a one-sided theory inhere in that term, we prefer to speak simply of elements . . . For us, therefore, the world does not consist of mysterious entities, which by interaction with another, equally mysterious entity, the ego, produce sensations, which alone are accessible. For us, colours, sounds, spaces, times . . . are provisionally the ultimate elements, whose given connection it is our business to investigate.

Such elements are, probably, what Wittgenstein usually has in mind as the ultimate constituents of the world; thus, in his article in the *Aristotelian Society Supplementary* (Vol. IX, 1929, p. 165), he says, 'If . . . we try to get at an actual analysis . . . we meet with   . . . colours, sounds, etc., with their gradations, continuous transitions, and combinations . . . all of which we cannot seize by our ordinary means of expression'. There are, of course, many and serious objections to the consideration of sense data as objects. For example, Wittgenstein speaks of possibility in connection with them (2.014); but it is senseless to speak of possibility in connection with a sense datum, because it is either actual or not at all, and modality does not apply to it. And is there any sense of speaking of the existence of sense data (2.027)? Yet it seems quite probable that Wittgenstein at times considers sense data—the ultimate data of our experience—as the ultimate elements into which the world is to be analyzable.

   1.212   The second meaning sometimes given to objects in the *Tractatus* is that of things. Thus Wittgenstein says, 'An atomic fact is a combination of objects (entities, things)' (2.01); and, even more specifically, 'spatial objects (such as

---

[5] Ernst Mach, *The Analysis of Sensations,* Open Court Publishing Company, Chicago, 1914. The quoted passages are from pp. 5, 22, and 29.

tables, chairs, books)' (3.1431). But 'The object is simple' (2.02), while things of everyday life are obviously complex, and thus while we may speak of things as objects in the sense of referends of the terms of our language, they cannot be considered as the ultimate elements of experience. And even if we decide that by objects Wittgenstein does not always mean the ultimate elements of the world, it would still be advisable not to use the terms 'things' and 'elements' interchangeably because these terms have different logical properties, and therefore our terminology should distinguish the two. Things are logical constructs involving hypotheses and are designed to express certain possible metrical relations among the elements of our experience, and they always take in our colloquial language the form of substantives. Thus, if we wish to speak of the ultimate constituents of our experience it would be better to use some such term as 'elements' to distinguish them from the constructs out of these elements, which may be then called 'things'. Of course, both 'elements' and 'things' are still pseudo-concepts because they do not stand for specific experiences or groups of experiences; they are only less inclusive than the term 'object', but in a perfect language they too would disappear.

1.213   So far my interpretation of 'object' has been in the empirical and positivistic spirit, but there also seems to be in the *Tractatus* signs of a metaphysical trend; at least Wittgenstein's terminology sometimes smacks of metaphysics. There seem to be two tendencies in the *Tractatus;* the major is positivistic, the minor metaphysical. Avowedly Wittgenstein is opposed to metaphysics and considers all metaphysics nonsensical, but occasionally he succumbs to the temptation and talks metaphysical nonsense; his treatment of 'object' is an example. It seems that at times he means by 'object' the ultimate ontological simple entities out of which the real world 'in itself' is made, something akin to Whitehead's 'objects' and Santayana's 'essences'; and, considering that Wittgenstein was influenced by Gottlob Frege, it may be that he is inclined toward a kind of Platonic realism. Thus Wittgenstein says, 'Objects form the substance of the world . . . what exists independently of what is the case' (2.021, 2.024), and it is suggested that it may be that we have no direct acquaintance with them (4.2211). But, as this metaphysical strain of Wittgenstein is not in accord with the general tenor of my interpretation of him, I will not pursue it here and will consider it as merely an unfortunate holdover from traditional metaphysical terminology.

1.214   To the three mentioned interpretations of 'object' we might add its interpretations as universals, determinables, determinates, and many others. But I see no advantage of pursuing this line of approach any further. The upshot of my discussion of 'object' so far is that there are no real entities specifically corresponding to the term 'object', and that Wittgenstein uses this term as a linguistic device for speaking about various kinds of entities, in particular the elements of sense data, common-life things, and ontological substances, all of which would not even appear in a perfect language. After these remarks I shall continue to use the term 'object' in the sense of 'referend' within our universe of discourse, and it will stand indiscriminately for the elements which are simple in relation to our language in actual use, as well as for logical constructs designed to express certain persistent or continuous relations between these elements; if I wish to distinguish between the two kinds I shall designate one as 'elements', the other as 'things'.

1.215   As an atomic fact is defined as a combination (2.01) or configuration (2.0272) of objects, the ambiguity and vagueness of what Wittgenstein means by objects leads inevitably to the similar uncertainty of the meaning of an atomic fact as well. Thus what is an atomic fact made up of things becomes a molecular and not atomic fact if considered as made up of elements of sense data. 'The pen is on the table' stands for an atomic fact if the pen and the table are taken as simple objects, as they usually are in everyday affairs; but the pen on the table is an indefinitely complex set of facts on a closer analysis. Thus, it is not at all clear what Wittgenstein means by atomic facts. It is quite probable that he means those facts which are apprehended directly in our perception and whose constituents are only simple sense data. But this is merely a probability, and the *Tractatus* does not give us any criterion for simplicity of sense data; therefore, even if we accept this interpretation, we are still at a loss for the precise meaning. The conclusion of my discussion of atomic facts as actual facts in the world is that I do not know what Wittgenstein means by atomic facts in this sense; I only guess that he may mean the simple facts whose constituents are only simple sense data, but I am at a loss for his criterion of simplicity in this connection. The approach to the meaning of the terms 'object' and 'atomic fact' through the discussion of the actual constitution of the world turns out to be decidely unprofitable.

1.22   And now I shall consider the objects and the atomic propositions from the second point of view (pp. 7–8); that is, I shall consider them from the point of view of the discussion of the formal requirements of any significant language and thus of any possible knowledge of the world, as contrasted with the previous discussion of them as the actual constituents of the world. We thus shall approach the objects and the atomic propositions through the discussions of names and atomic propositions.

1.221   The theoretical need of atomic propositions and simple terms or names arises from the formal requirements for determinateness of sense and meaning. A given proposition will have a determinate sense only if in our analysis of the proposition we can come to the propositions whose sense does not further depend upon any other propositions, and the meaning of whose terms requires no further reduction to the meaning of any other terms. And these last propositions and terms are called respectively atomic propositions and names. A composite proposition is a function of its constituent propositions (*Tractatus*, 5), and therefore can have sense only if these propositions have sense; thus in looking for the sense of a composite proposition we come to the relatively simple propositions. But, finally, if our analysis is to give us a determinate sense, we must get to atomic propositions, that is, those which have no other propositions as constituents and whose sense, therefore, must be determined not by any further reduction to other propositions but by direct reference to the facts in the world. 'Propositions can be true or false only by being pictures of the reality' (4.06). And the facts expressed by these atomic propositions are the corresponding atomic facts (4.21). 'One name stands for one thing, and another thing . . . And so the whole, like a living picture, presents the atomic fact' (4.0311).

And an atomic proposition in its turn, if it is to have sense, must be constituted of primitive terms or names with fixed meanings in our experience, that is, terms which we do not define by other terms, but which stand as signals for determinate elements within our experience. 'The name cannot be analysed further by any definition. It is a primitive sign' (3.26). Otherwise we could analyze the propositions in which they occur still further into a product of other propositions, and the atomicity of the original proposition would not be real. The proposition 'This is a table' may be roughly analyzed into 'This has a flat top, and this has four legs, and . . .', which is obviously not an atomic proposition; in this case the term 'table' obviously is not a simple term. Thus, if we are to have sensible atomic propositions we must have simple terms or names. 'The postulate of the possibility of the simple signs is the postulate of the determinateness of the sense' (3.23).

A question still may arise here: Why should not we arbitrarily take atomic propositions themselves as our simple or primitive symbols? The answer is that, if we did so, the very senses of our propositions, and not only their truth values, would depend upon the actual state of affairs in the world.

If we stopped with atomic propositions as our primitive signs, then in order to have significant propositions we would have to have specific atomic facts corresponding to these atomic propositions; that is, we would need specific fixed configurations in the world before we could even give determinate sense to our propositions.

In order to state sensible propositions we would have to learn beforehand what atomic facts there are; that is, we would have to know the state of affairs in the world. In other words, we could not use false atomic propositions, just as we cannot have meaningless names; and our true atomic propositions would play the logical role of names— a view of Frege's rejected by Wittgenstein (3.143, 4.061, 5.02).

Thus, according to Wittgenstein, if the formal requirements of significant language are to be met, there must be: (a) *names* or fixed simple primitive symbols, that is, symbols undefinable in terms of any other symbols but directly indicating the fixed elements of our experience; and (b) simple or *atomic propositions,* that is, propositions consisting of concatenations of names and not containing any propositions as constituents. Atomic propositions actually describe atomic facts by using names (and not descriptions) which indicate the elements constituting the corresponding atomic facts. And if our language is to be significant in the world, there must be simple elements or objects which we could name, and atomic facts which we could describe.

1.222   An objection may be raised at this point to this mode of procedure of discussing atomic facts and their elements via atomic propositions and names. It may be said that we are putting the cart before the horse by discussing atomic propositions about facts in order to come to an understanding of the facts themselves—that we seem to decree to reality what features it should possess. In a word we may be accused of dogmatic rationalism, the essence of which is the doctrine that reason is the source of real knowledge of the world.

The answer to this very serious objection is that we are not making any significant statements about the world, but are discussing the fundamental conditions of all significant symbolism applicable to any world. However, on one hand the formal requirements of symbolism cannot dictate the nature of reality, but on the other hand—and this is of the utmost importance in Wittgenstein's view—we cannot discuss a reality which does not conform to the necessary prerequisites of all symbolism, because we cannot have any discussion (and therefore knowledge) without the medium of symbolism. There is no sense in discussing reality unless it is describable in a language, and it cannot be describable unless its features conform to the formal requirements of all symbolism. We have here a sort of Kantian phenomenalism in Wittgenstein. 'Logic is transcendental' (6.13), and the similarity is, I believe, more than merely verbal.

But a warning must be made here. On one hand, to say that it is nonsensical to discuss reality if it does not conform to the prerequisites of language is not the same as to deny any reality. We cannot deny what we cannot discuss. We simply refuse to describe what is, by definition, undescribable; we refuse to talk nonsense. That reality is not confined to the describable is admitted by Wittgenstein in his 'mystical'. But on the other hand, to state the necessary conditions of significant language is not equivalent to an assertion that there *is* a reality conforming to these conditions. That again would be talking nonsense. That there is such a reality as organized by our language activity is a fact of experience and does not follow from merely formal requirements of language. It does not follow from anything, for that matter, but simply *is* the case, and might have been not the case without in the least affecting the formal requirements of symbolism. Of course, there would not have been then any actual language, and I would not be discussing now even the formal prerequisites of an ideal language, but that has nothing to do with these formal prerequisites themselves.

1.223   The résumé of my discussion so far is that our language must have simple, meaningful terms or *names* and simple or atomic propositions with determinate sense. The names stand for simple elements or objects in our world; and the *atomic propositions* describe the configurations of these elements, that is, *atomic facts*. If our language is to be significant of the world there must be in the world elements for which the names stand, and atomic facts described by true atomic propositions. These requirements are formal; they have to be met by any language, and they do not say anything specific about our world.

1.3   The question now arises how the above formal requirements are to be complied with even by an ideal language in *application* within the world; and that leads us to the problem of the connection between language and reality. We may consider this as the epistemological problem approached by the way of language. And here again the discussion is to be as far as possible on a nonempirical level. The fundamental problem here is not so much that of the application of the formal requirements of language in our actual world, but of the formal conditions necessary for application in any possible world, of the conditions to be met by any knowledge. We may call this the problem of the grammar of language, and of thought as well. It is merely the extension of our discussion of the purely formal requirements of symbolism to the formal requirements of its possible application.

1.31   A significant language, we have decided, requires simple elements and atomic facts in the world, the first to be named, the second to be stated by atomic propositions. Now we are to consider the conditions necessary to meet these formal requirements in application in the world; and, more specifically, I am now raising the question of how we are to decide in the actual use of language in the world whether a certain element in our experience is simple or not, or whether a certain fact is atomic or molecular. I have already indirectly touched upon this problem in the earlier part of this chapter, and came to the conclusion that the *Tractatus* is not at all clear about what is to be meant by the simple elements or objects, and consequently what are the atomic facts. Among various alternatives, all very problematic, I have suggested that the sense data may be taken as the simple elements, because this view seems to be in accord with the general tenor of Wittgenstein's teaching, especially after the publication of the *Tractatus*. But it is very pertinent to ask what criterion we are to use in testing our experience for simples. *I do not find in the Tractatus any satisfactory criterion for simplicity*, and I think this is due to the fact that Wittgenstein himself is not clear as to what he means by the limit of analysis. 'There is one and only one complete analysis of the proposition' (3.25), and this analysis is not arbitrary (3.3442). But how are we to decide in any given case whether the analysis has been completed or not? And what assurance do we have that if pursued long enough (how long?) it will come to the one and the only one end?

Shall we take our psychological limitations as the criteria —shall we say that our inability to analyze something any further is equivalent to its being unanalyzable? But in that case we have either to give up the second characteristic of the 'object', namely, its fixity (2.027), or else to postulate an absolute and fixed limit to our psychological ability to analyze. The first alternative has to be rejected because it would destroy the determinateness of our language; and the second is useless without some further criterion to enable us to decide in any given case whether we have reached the postulated limit of psychological capacity to analyze. The natural criterion here might be the self-evidence of having arrived at such a limit. But self-evidence as a criterion is definitely rejected by Wittgenstein; 'obviousness is no justification for our belief' (5.1363). He accuses even Frege of falling a victim to using self-evidence as a criterion. Of course, Wittgenstein himself does not escape using this criterion either

in his occasional confuson of psychological 'cannot' with logical 'impossible', as I shall show later; but, nevertheless, in
principle he rejects it. A psychological criterion then must be
rejected, and I can find no other in the *Tractatus*.

Sometimes it seems that Wittgenstein speaks of the absolute
limits of analyses of data of experience independent of our
psychic powers. 'Even if the world is infinitely complex, so
that every fact consists of an infinite number of atomic facts
and every atomic fact is composed of an infinite number of
objects, even then there must be objects and atomic facts'
(4.2211). The fact that we have no means of detecting such
hidden ontological entities and facts and, therefore, have no
means of applying language to them, is, of course, irrelevant
to a metaphysician. But for us the problem of connecting
language with reality, the problem of significant language,
still remains. (This is roughly the setting of Kant's problem in
the *Critique of Pure Reason*.) We are still left without a
criterion for recognition of the needed simple elements and,
therefore, without means of using language significantly. I do
not propose, however, to pursue the investigation of Wittgenstein's metaphysical vagaries; that is the weakness and not the
important side of the *Tractatus* as I interpret it.

The upshot of these remarks is that we are left without
criteria for simplicity, and thus without means of applying
in the world the formal requirements of significant language.
But then these requirements themselves become useless, and
in application to our world meaningless. Of course, even if
we had the needed criterion, we still might find difficulty in
applying it in practice. But such difficulty would be merely
practical; on the other hand, the lack of any criterion leads
tautologically to the impossibility of applying it.

It is no wonder then that even such people as Russell and
Ramsey find it difficult to exhibit an actual case of an atomic
proposition! The situation is analogous to the one confronted
by the League of Nations in 1932 in its attempt to decide
who was the aggressor in the Sino-Japanese conflict; the

League's decision had to be based on considerations logically irrelevant to the question raised, because the question itself was senseless without a definite criterion for aggression.

Some criterion is indispensable here. And my contention, which I shall defend a little later, is that *any criterion or rule of simplicity whatsoever is to be arbitrarily assigned* by ourselves, and that there is nothing in reality to impose upon us any rule. It is then senseless to look in reality for a criterion of simplicity, and therefore for what is to be the element and what atomic fact in our experience. To make this clear we have to discuss in somewhat more detail the role of language in our knowledge of the world.

1.32   Language is the activity in which we use some parts of our experience to stand for or signify certain other parts of our experience. And the result of such an activity is a world. 'We make to ourselves pictures of facts' (2.1), and the picture itself is also a fact (2.141)—the fact that 'its elements are combined with one another in a definite way' (2.14). Thus, when actually used, 'the gramophone record, the musical thought, the score, the waves of sound, all stand to one another in that pictorial internal relation, which holds between language and the world' (4.014). Until so interrelated and interpreted, our experience is not the world. All our experience and knowledge of the world is through language in this wide sense of the word; there can be no other world for us besides the one that is organized on our own terms, and thus there can be no world for us except as understood through language. '*The limits of my language* mean the limits of my world' (5.6); 'to give the essence of proposition means to give the essence of all description, therefore the essence of the world' (5.4711). Wittgenstein's view on language is a version of Kant's 'Copernican revolution in philosophy'.

Which parts of experience we shall use as symbols and which as symbolized is logically arbitrary, and in practice the choice is directed by tradition, convenience, or even merely by accident. There is no necessity of calling a certain object 'cabbage' or 'chou' any more than 'Kohl' or 'kapusta' or anything else. We naturally tend to take the less bulky and more handy things to be the symbols, but even that is not always the case. As Whitehead points out in his profound little book, *Symbolism,* a poet in the throes of composing a poem may very well use the trees in the woods to stand as symbols for the words of the poem he is composing; as Whitehead puts it (p. 12), 'He concentrates on the trees in order to get at the words'. Theoretically it is irrelevant what parts of our experience are used as the material of symbols; they very well may be 'made up of spatial objects (such as tables, chairs, books) instead of written signs' (3.1431). Thus, what is to be a symbol and what symbolized depends upon the functional relationship of the facts and elements within our world, and this relationship is determined by the language activity and is relative to the conceptual base of the language as chosen in that activity. It is almost needless to add that for Wittgenstein the symbols need not be mental. In fact ideas and images are in many ways less satisfactory as symbols than, for instance, letters, because they are more vague and fleeting than letters.

No absolute fixed once-and-for-all separation could be established between language and the world within which the language is being used. It is a common mistake of both rationalists and traditional empiricists completely to separate language (in their terminology, mind) from the world. Language interrelates the factors of our experience; without such interrelation no experience of the world is possible, and it is senseless to try to discuss impossible experiences; yet without there being a world, language would be also impossible. To put it in a different way: without thought (for Wittgenstein equivalent to language) the objects of thought would be meaningless, and then the world without being thought about would be, tautologically, meaningless; but without a world there would be no activity which is thinking, therefore no thought, no language. To ask what is language in this broad sense apart from reality and what is reality apart from language, is to err in the very formulation of the question. We should ask instead: What shall we look upon as language and what as reality? And in dealing with this question our principle must be not to make any sweeping universal metaphysical assertions, but always to stop with the concrete situations within our world. It is we who make to ourselves the picture of facts in our world. Language can be used only within the region determined by the language itself. We must not think of language as if devised by a being entirely apart from the world, as if a philosophical tailor were taking some cosmological measures for a categorical costume of an ontological customer entirely apart and distinct from the self-contained tailor, as well as from the character of the measuring appliances used.

One of the things we must avoid in discussing this problem of the relation between language and the world is the tendency to look for absolute entities or realities in what we mean or refer to. What is actually meant is to be determined in each particular case by the language activity itself within the given context, and we must not speak about once-and-for-all-fixed 'reality in itself' to which we must refer in the last analysis each and all of our propositions. When I say 'I have a headache', it is my headache that is meant as it is understood by my family or acquaintances or a doctor; and within the context in which I use this expression it has definite even though not very precise meaning; it is sufficiently meaningful to my friend, who suggests that I take an aspirin tablet; no question of the ultimate reality of my headache or of aspirin arises. Again, when we refer in astronomy to 'the other side of the moon' our meaning is clear to the astronomers within the context of their scientific conventions. 'There is a chair in the next room' is a false but meaningful proposition within the context of everyday speech if there is no chair in the next room. By there being no chair in the next room we mean, on the level of everyday context, that if we go into the next room we shall find no chair there; we know how to verify this proposition, and this knowing raises no further problems. In the case of Caesar's death (whether by murder or illness in bed) the procedure is more complicated but is again determined by the historian's conventions of how to deal with past events. In each case here we know within the actual concrete context what is the symbol and what is the symbolized; the meanings here are clear and unambiguous even if not entirely precise; and no problem of the ultimate realities arises.

All this does not, of course, mean that language and the world are identical (in the language of traditional idealism, that thought and being are the same); it means only that without language we could have no connected, systematic experience, no world. While our language determines the scope of meaningful discourse, and thus limits the possibilities within our world, it does not and cannot determine the existence or nonexistence of anything within the world. As Anatole France remarked, 'The most scientific system of numbering will not help us to find a book if the book is no longer in its place'. What actually is in the world has to be found by observation and cannot be deduced from the formal requirements of language. 'What lies in its application logic cannot anticipate' (*Tractatus*, 5.557); 'There is no order of things a priori' (5.634). The truth of a proposition does not depend on the language but on the actual state of affairs in the world. Wittgenstein holds the correspondence theory of truth. 'In order to discover whether the picture is true or false we must compare it with reality' (2.223). But we need no metaphysics here, no 'external reality' outside the limits of our experience. Both the pictures and what is pictured exist in the same sense; both are facts and equally real. We compare the proposition and the fact it expresses within the same world, but 'It cannot be discovered from the picture alone whether it is true or false' (2.224). 'There is no picture which is a priori true' (2.225).

Perhaps we might introduce here merely for convenience of discussion a terminological distinction between event and fact in order to discriminate between that aspect of our experience which is not affected by language, the objective aspect, so to say, and the aspect contributed by language. An event when it is fitted into the schema of discourse becomes a fact. We cannot discuss sheer events. The proposition 'The pen is on the table' describes the fact that the pen is on the table; and this proposition cannot be true unless there is an event which can be organized within our system of language into the fact of the pen's being on the table; but we could not describe the mere event without its being formulated into a fact. Events are what just happen; facts are events formulated within our system of language, within our universe of discourse. I shall not, however, adhere to this terminological distinction because Wittgenstein himself does not make it, and will continue to use the term 'fact' to cover both.

1.33   And now we can return to the discussion of the formal conditions necessary for the application of language in a possible world, that is, to the problem of grammar, which we left (p. 20) at the discussion of the criteria of simplicity in order to discuss the connection between language and reality. By grammar in this wide sense of the term we are to understand any set of rules governing the use of symbolism.

1.331   It is important to note that *grammar logically precedes the application* of symbolism: 'Logic *precedes* every experience—that something is *so*' (5.552). Before we can use symbols we must determine their meaning, but 'the determination . . . is *only a description of symbols and asserts nothing about what is symbolized*' (3.317). 'It is before the How, not before the What' (5.552). That the rules of grammar are not empirical propositions is obvious from the fact that there is no sense in raising a question of truth or falsity of a rule of grammar. 'In order to know an object, I must know not its external but all its internal qualities' (2.01231). The internal or formal qualities or properties are the qualities determining the concept of the object, the qualities without which the object cannot be thought of, the qualities which we can deduce from the very concept of this object; 'a property is internal if it is unthinkable that its object does not possess it' (4.123). In a word, internal properties are those that belong to the grammar of the term. External properties are those that are merely factual or empirical, those that have no effect on the concept of the object, do not belong to the grammar of the term. It is an internal property of a pen that it can be used as an instrument in writing; but whether it is a fountain pen or a goose quill, black, white, or green are external properties of the pen. Thus, the meaning of a symbol is known from its grammar, which is assigned to the symbol. And if we know the grammar of a symbol we know how to use the symbol in language; the grammar of a symbol determines the range of its applicability: 'if a thing *can* occur in an atomic fact the possibility of that atomic fact must already be prejudged in the thing' (2.012). The possible logically precedes the actual.

1.332   Here I must insert a few remarks on the much-discussed subject of possibility. 'Possible' is for Wittgenstein what is expressible in language: 'The picture contains the possibility of the state of affairs which it represents' (2.203). 'The thought contains the possibility of the state of affairs which it thinks. What is thinkable is also possible' (3.02). 'Possible' refers to the scope of the language, to what Wittgenstein calls the 'logical space', and therefore includes the actual facts in the world insofar as what is actual in our world must be expressible in our language. What is actual in the world is also expressible or possible, but the possible is not necessarily actual: 'Every thing is, as it were, in a space of possible atomic facts. I can think of the space as empty, but not of the thing without the space' (2.013). The grammar of our language draws the limits to the possible; the objects of our language 'contain the possibility of all states of affairs' (2.014). The objects of our thought cannot occur without their grammar; when we apply language to reality we do not have to discover what property a certain thing has in reality, but just the reverse: first we assign the properties which the thing is to have and only then try to recognize in reality the thing whose properties we have assigned. 'If I know an object, then I also know all the possibilities of its occurrence in atomic facts. . . . A new possibility cannot subsequently be found' (2.0123); 'If things can occur in atomic facts, this possibility must already lie in them' (2.0121); 'if a thing *can* occur in an atomic fact the possibility of that atomic fact must already be prejudged in the thing' (2.012). Grammar logically is prior to the application. This view of possibility is essentially that of Hume: 'Whatever the mind clearly conceives includes the idea of possible existence, or in other words, that nothing we imagine is absolutely impossible' (*Treatise*, Selby-Bigge ed., p. 32). Wittgenstein differs from Hume in lifting the problem from the psychological confines of Hume's treatment. Possibility on this view has meaning only in discourse, and refers to the scope of the symbolism. 'Sheer events in themselves' are outside discourse, and possibility and impossibility cannot apply to them. There seems to be another kind of possibility, however, which is considered as residing in some way in the nature of things themselves regardless of our actual knowledge about them. But if there were such a 'possibility' in our world, it still must be at least knowable, that is, expressible by our language; otherwise it is utter nonsense to us. It is then something to be determined by observation within the world, that is, within the power of symbolization of our language. In short, this latter 'possibility' is then but another name for an empirical law of nature. When we say that something is possible in this sense we simply mean that it is within the law of regularity of nature as postulated on the basis of observation and experimentation. We may distinguish various degrees of this so-called 'possibility' in the extent and the specificity of the field under consideration, ranging from the possibility that the laws of physics will hold tomorrow to the possibility that there is a chair in the next room. But discussion of this distinction is entirely outside the task of this book. This second use of the term 'possibility' is narrower than and is included in the first meaning. Our natural laws are propositions or, rather, models for making propositions, and therefore are always expressible in our language. But our language can express more than a natural law would allow.

An illustration may help to clarify the view of possibility I am trying to explain. A little boy, my neighbor, insists that my wife is my mother. While this is a grave moral indictment, it is logically quite possible. It could be true, and then it would be theoretically possible for my friend to substantiate his accusation. That it happens to be false as a matter of fact does not detract from its possibility. So far my little friend makes a significant, even though false, statement. But he goes farther and makes another statement, significant if taken by itself, even though again false, namely, that I am my wife's father. Now, while either of these statements if taken alone describes a possible situation, yet when they are made in conjunction (as "I am my mother's husband and I am my wife's father"), the result is a self-contradictory statement, and cannot possibly describe an actual situation in the world. In order to defend myself against my friend's accusation of double moral turpitude, I do not have to appeal to the facts of my biography or any other facts in the world, as I would have to do if he contented himself with either one of his single accusations. All I have to do now in order to refute him is to show that his accusation is self-contradictory and therefore what he says about me is impossible; and I can do that by merely pointing out that the grammar of the words 'father', 'mother', 'wife', and 'husband' makes it impossible to make a significant proposition out of the sentence 'I am my mother's husband and I am my wife's father'. The impossibility follows from the grammar of our language. A still simpler illustration is that of the 'round square'. It is possible to have round things, and it is possible to have square things, but it is impossible to have round-squared things; and for finding out the possibilities and the impossibility here we do not have to go to experience but merely examine the grammar of our language.

The subject of possibility is interesting and important, but I will not pursue it here any further. I have inserted this short discussion in order to make clearer the statement that the grammatical determination logically precedes the application of language in the world, and now we can return to the interrupted discussion of that topic.

1.333   It is very important in Wittgenstein's view that the grammar logically precedes the application of language in the world, and therefore we cannot deduce grammatical rules of our language from experience any more than we can deduce a standard of measure (which is also a rule, of course) from our spatial experience. Of course the determination of grammar may be affected by practical considerations, but that is logically irrelevant. We may, for example, find it convenient to use the length of man's foot as a measure because we find rigid bodies to be readily measurable by the foot as a standard of measure. But before the foot becomes the standard it must be chosen to be the standard. This determination does not depend on the fact that there are many or any things to which this standard can be conveniently applied; and it is merely an accident that the original standard measure happened to be the actual foot of some prehistoric geometer. The original foot of the original geometer was not so measured before the man decided to consider it to be the standard; and thus his foot was not of the length of one foot before the original decision. It is only after the foot was chosen as the standard that it became the standard, something fixed within the language of the geometer, to be used in measuring spatial objects, including his own feet. We choose our standard and its rules arbitrarily before we can use it. But on the other hand this standard has a significance in the world: by means of this standard we know how to measure the world, and the results will not be arbitrary.

This priority or independence of the grammar from experience is *logical and not psychological* or in any other sense empirical. Aristotle said: 'Now "prior" and "better known" are ambiguous terms, for there is a difference between what is prior and better known in the order of being and what is prior and better known to man' (*Posterior Analytics*, 71ᵇ30). If we change 'the order of being' to 'the determination of grammar', this passage expresses the distinction drawn here between the logical and the psychological or empirical. The grammar of language cannot be deduced from experience, even though experience may, and often does as a matter of fact, precede temporally the formation of particular rules. 'We can know *a priori* of things only what we ourselves put into them', as Kant said (*Critique of Pure Reason,* Bxviii).

This distinction may be also expressed by the contrast between the *ground* or reason embodied in a rule and the *causes* which lead us to adopt the rule in practice. The causal connections are always hypothetical and are to be established empirically; the grounds of a rule are categorical and are established within language, are merely linguistic assertions. The cause and the ground express two entirely different meanings of the status of a rule. The cause is to be ascertained by experience, and may be confirmed or refuted by experience; the ground is given in the rule itself, and before we can apply it. A rule would be a rule even if there were no causal connections in the world. The rule is purely discursive and cannot be found in experience as a calf with ten legs could be found.

Let us take as an example the reading aloud of an English book. Why do we pronounce words as we do? On one hand

I can give a causal explanation: my nerves are stimulated by the sight of these letters in such a way that I make certain noises, and my nervous reaction is conditioned by my training. This explanation may be, of course, false in detail. But a similar explanation could also be given for any mechanism able to perform such a feat; and, while we do not deny that our organisms may be reacting mechanically in our behavior, the causal explanation of our behavior does not give us any account of the rules of the English language. It explains the causal connection between letters and the sounds I make upon seeing the letters, but it is not concerned with any rules or with conformity to them. On the other hand, if someone asked me why I pronounce certain letters as I do, I would answer, not with a description of the processes in my nervous system and of my training, but with a rule. The distinction here is logical: the character of my behavior follows from the rule, not in the sense of being caused by it, as the talking of a phonograph is caused by my turning the switch, but in the sense that the character of my behavior conforms to the rule. If asked for a rule, we state a rule. And if asked by what we are guided in acknowledging this rule, we refer to some other rule, and not to experience. If we are pressed, eventually we shall have to stop, however, and merely 'show' the rule by using it in a concrete case.

The case of language is the same as the case of any game—chess, for example. We do not gather the rules of the game from the actions of the players in the sense that we gather the laws of astronomy from observation of the stars. The difference is due to the fact that the rules of chess are not empirical propositions to be confirmed or refuted by the moves of an actual game. The rules would be the same if no one ever played the game, or if all the players were always cheating and not conforming to the rules. The result of our observation of the players would be: 'They play in such and such a way'. This would be an empirical proposition about the action of the players; it would not be a statement of the rules of chess, because the rules of chess are rules and not the natural laws of behavior of the chess players as gathered from observation of the players. It may, of course, happen that the laws derived from prolonged observation of the movements of the chessmen in actual games will completely coincide with the rules of chess. But the fundamental distinction between grammatical rules and laws obtained from observation will still hold: rules are in principle fixed a priori and once for all before the game can be played, while the empirical laws are gathered from experience, are hypotheses, and may be refuted by experience. Certain rules may be logically prerequisite for having the type of experience we happen to have. But it is not logically necessary that there should have been such experiences as we do have, and with different rules of organizing the raw data we could have had a different type of experience. 'That a picture . . . can be described by a network of a given form asserts *nothing* about the picture. (For this holds for every picture of this kind.) But *this* does characterize the picture, . . . that it can be *completely* described by a definite net of *definite* fineness' (6.342). The question "What is the rule?" is the question about the determination of the use of the symbols or objects, and therefore it will not be answered by the facts of experience, but only by the description of the rules for the use of the symbols before the symbols can be used. In the terminology of Wittgenstein it will be answered by what language 'shows' and not by what it 'says'. We must understand the internal or grammatical properties of our language before we can make any practical use of it, before 'saying' anything. 'The determination will . . . deal only with symbols not with . . . *what is symbolized*' (3.317).

Kant thought that the rules indispensable for the human experience are fixed a priori forms of our 'knowing faculty'. For Wittgenstein they are the rules of grammar of our language by means of which we organize our experience. With this essential difference, Kant's opening statements in the

Introduction to his *Critique of Pure Reason* fits in well with Wittgenstein's view as I interpret it here:

All our knowledge begins with experience . . . But . . . it does not follow that it all arises out of experience. For it may well be that even our empirical knowledge is made up of what we receive thru impressions and of what our own faculty of knowledge . . . supplies from itself . . . it may be that we are not in a position to distinguish it from the raw material until with long practice of attention we have become skilled in separating it (*Critique of Pure Reason,* Bi).

Incidentally, the confusion between the formal meaning of rules and the natural laws is the source of the blunders committed by those philosophers who, like J. S. Mill, hold that logic and mathematics are based upon experience and not upon the rules of symbolism.

1.34   The view on language and its grammar just presented is, I believe, essentially and on the whole what was intended to be presented in the *Tractatus*. Assuming that my account of Wittgenstein here is correct, I will criticize him for not adhering to his own view on certain occasions. Wittgenstein is guilty, I believe, of confusing at times the psychological capacity with logical necessity, of certain empirical considerations with the logical grounds of grammatical rules. Wittgenstein is aware of the danger of confusing psychology with logic: 'Does not my study of sign-language correspond to the study of thought processes which philosophers held to be so essential to the philosophy of logic? Only they got entangled for the most part in unessential psychological investigations, and there is an analogous danger for my method' (4.1121). In spite of this, however, Wittgenstein did get entangled in psychology or at any rate with empirical considerations, even if not 'for the most part'. As an example, we can take his discussion of color.

1.341   Wittgenstein says: 'A speck in a visual field need not be red, but it must have a colour; it has, so to speak, a colour space round it' (2.0131). Considering the abstruseness of Wittgenstein's style and his fondness for metaphors, a favorable interpretation of this passage might be that it is merely a sketchy description of the grammar of the terms 'red', 'colour', and 'space', and not at all a description of psychological experiences of colors. This interpretation seems to be substantiated by the first paragraph of 6.3751: 'For two colours, *e.g.*, to be at one place in the visual field, is . . . logically impossible, for it is excluded by the logical structure of colour', where by the logical structure we may mean the grammar of color. But, unfortunately, the second paragraph of the same 6.3751 makes such interpretation too strained: 'Let us consider how this contradiction presents itself in physics. Somewhat as follows: That a particle cannot at the same time have two velocities, *i.e.*, that at the same time it cannot be in two places, *i.e.*, that particles in different places at the same time cannot be identical'. Here Wittgenstein tries to reduce color to the physicist's account of it. But physics is for Wittgenstein an empirical science (3.0321), and thus he tries to reduce his account of color to empirical laws. Whether in our analysis of color we stop with physical or psychological laws, we are in either case dealing with experience and not with the rules of language; the grammar of color is then treated as a natural law about psychological or physical experiences, and not as a set of rules of language determined independently of the actual state of affairs in the world.

1.342   But my criticism of Wittgenstein here goes even farther. The natural laws, if we treat them as derived from empirical observation, cannot give the fixity required by the rules. To give them this fixity we would have to treat them as revealing certain fixity in nature itself. The experience of facts does not, however, furnish us with the fixity required by language, and so we postulate something fixed and hidden behind the experience, which we draw out and embody in the grammar of our language. Here, again, we discern a metaphysical streak in Wittgenstein.

To illustrate this we might use a simile. Let us imagine rigid bodies, say cubes, made of some invisible material, say solidified air, and each painted only on one face. Let us assume that we are restricted to visual experiences; we shall then be able to experience only the colored squares but not the other parts of the cubes. Let us assume that we can move the colored squares about. We will find that we cannot move the colored squares entirely arbitrarily; that is so, of course, because the invisible cubes of which the squares are the faces prevent certain movements. From the experience of moving these squares we may derive a law for the motion of colored squares, which may lead to a postulate that there are invisible cubes attached to each of our squares and that our laws of the possible relations of colored squares in space are due to the properties of the invisible cubes. Our laws are conditioned by something which is, by hypothesis, beyond our experience. We are talking metaphysics.

Wittgenstein the metaphysician seems to imply that there is something inexperienceable in nature and that the fixed grammar of color is due to this hidden something with its own properties. This view has to be, of course, rejected on the positivistic interpretation of the *Tractatus*. What is, by hypothesis, inexperienceable is, tautologically, meaningless and is ruled out of discussion. But let us change the simile a little. Let us reject the metaphysical bodies, and instead of them postulate fixed and permanent relations between the colored squares, and then consider the rules of grammar of the colored squares as natural laws depicting these fixed relations. The fixity of relations is then a scientific hypothesis based on some empirical evidence, and so it does not convey any logical fixity or necessity. And if we decide to consider these relations as fixed, then they become rules of our language. The laws of the possibility of spatial arrangements of the colored squares are nothing but grammatical rules. Whether they correspond or not to our experience is another and practical matter.

We cannot actually separate, but we still must distinguish, the grammar of colors from the facts of our experiencing color. Regardless of the origin, usefulness, and even empirically invariable coordination of this grammar with experience, we must not consider the grammatical rules as registrations of empirical observations. The necessity we find in the properties of color (for example, that it is impossible for what is red also to be green) is a necessity of rules, of the internal or logical properties of the concept of color, and not of the facts. There is no necessity in facts; facts simply are or are not, 'and everything else remain[s] the same' (1.21). Necessity is only formal or logical, that of following consistently the accepted rules of language as long as we use language, and 'There is only a *logical* necessity . . . only a *logical* impossibility' (6.375). It is the same necessity as that of following the rules of a game, if we are to play the game. We do not have to play chess, but if we do, then we must conform to the rules of chess; and if we do not conform, we are simply not playing chess but doing something else. It is logically impossible to play the game without following the rules.

1.343   An objection may be offered here that there is a fundamental difference between the experiences of seeing color and of playing chess. We find that, whether we like it or not, the grammar of color is empirically unavoidable in actual dealing with our visual experiences, while we can very well make up another set of rules for the chessmen, and play some other kind of game with the same pieces on the same board. It seems that there is some necessity, besides a merely formal one, for our rules in the grammar of color, and that this necessity is in some sense dictated by experience. But this objection is based on the confusion of the 'cannot' of experience with the 'impossible' of language. The coincidence of the 'cannot' of experience with the 'impossible' of the grammar of color is purely empirical and therefore accidental. Even in the game of chess there are such point-to-point correspondences of the empirical 'cannot' and logical 'impossible'; we cannot, as it is also impossible for us, have one and the same chesspiece in two places at once. The grammar of the physical body here coincides with the uniformity of our tactual experience. The fact that our grammar or color accompanies all the empirically observed structures of visual experience must not mislead us into thinking that the necessity we find here is due to experience. The necessity lies only in our grammar and not in our psychological experience. What experience establishes, experience may also destroy. The complete adequacy of the grammar in its application to experience in the case of color is but an accident and is logically irrelevant to the necessity of grammar. There is no impossibility of a sudden change in my psychic or physiological capacity. Perhaps tomorrow, like a multi-eyed insect, I shall be able to see what I call now red and green on one and the same patch. I shall then still be able to have my old grammar with its impossibility of seeing red and green together, but it will no longer be adequate to deal with my new color experiences. Perhaps my old grammar may become quite useless in application, just as some systems of geometry may be useless. I may then try to invent a new grammar to meet the new experiences; it may even happen that the new experiences will be so chaotic that I shall not be able to construct a grammar applicable to them, and then my experiences will be outside my discourse, and therefore outside my world. In fact it is nonsense to talk about my future experiences to which my present grammar does not, by definition, apply, even if I should become able at some future time to invent a new grammar to fit that sense experience. It will be quite a different world. But to come back to our present experiences of color, we can say that the fact that we cannot imagine any other structure of our visual experience except the one we actually do imagine makes all the discussion of different visual experiences meaningless at present. But it does not make the actual structure necessary. It is quite possible that there could be no color experience at all.

1.344   Thus, 'grammatical determination' is any logically arbitrary determination to use signs in certain ways. We may make here a distinction between two kinds of grammatical rules. Rules of *one kind* remain, so to speak, completely within the grammar of language; we may, perhaps, say that they deal merely with the purely logical syntax of language, and 'must admit of being established without mention being thereby made of the *meaning* of a sign' (3.33). They deal with the so-called logical constants, such as 'or', 'and', 'not', 'if', and so on, which do not stand for anything in the world (4.0312, 5.4). They are not names with meanings. Thus the syntax of 'not' says that a double negation is equivalent to an assertion. 'Not' is not a name for anything in reality: 'The sign "~" corresponds to nothing in reality . . . The propositions "p" and "$\sim p$" have opposite senses, but to them corresponds one and the same reality' (4.0621); 'The proposition "$\sim \sim p$" does not treat of denial as an object' (5.44). Wittgenstein uses the term 'negative fact' (2.06), but this seems hardly more than a linguistic device; negation is needed in language only because we cannot as a matter of fact give a complete description of the world. If we were omniscient and omnipotent and used a perfect language we would have no need of negation or of any other 'logical constants': 'there are no such things as . . . "logical constants" ' (5.4). [Wittgenstein, unfortunately, is not quite consistent on this point (5.511, 5.512).] Rules of *the other kind* deal with the symbols designed for dealing with the world of experience: 'The possibility of propositions is based upon the principle of representation of objects by signs' (4.0312). These rules establish *meaning* of symbols in terms of our experience, and are established by what W. E. Johnson calls 'ostensive definition'. Thus, for example, I can say: 'These → colors I will call *red*', or 'red' → $\boxed{\substack{\text{red} \\ \text{patch}}}$. Both of these kinds of rules are included in the grammar of language, and are determined logically independently of experience, in contrast to the *use* of language when we wish to express something about the actual state of affairs in the world. The grammar of the language is fixed once and for all; its use in making propositions varies from case to case.

1.4   After this long digression on the nature of language and its connection with the world, we can return now to the discussion of the problem of objects and atomic facts. We have found (pp. 13 ff.) that we need simple elements and simple atomic facts in order to meet the formal requirements of any significant language for meaningful names and true atomic propositions. But we have found in the *Tractatus* no criterion for what is to be considered as simple in the application of these formal requirements to the actual use of language (p. 17). It becomes now obvious that, in the view here expounded, it is logically perfectly arbitrary what we shall choose to consider as simple elements and atomic facts; the criterion of simplicity is to be established by ourselves, not found in the world. The practical considerations of convenience, habit, or usefulness may, of course, guide us in our grammatical determinations, but are logically irrelevant.

1.41   The simple symbols of a significant language are called names: 'The simple signs employed in propositions are called names' (3.202). The formal definition of a simple symbol is that it must have no parts which are symbols themselves: 'no sort of composition [is] essential for a name' (3.3411). The mere physical appearance of the sign is accidental; what determines the simplicity of the symbol is the definition or the grammar of the symbol. Thus the sign $f(a)$ may be considered either simple or complex, depending on the rules agreed upon. If different rules are valid for f and for a, then the symbol $f(a)$ is complex; if the rules refer to $f(a)$ as a simple unit symbol, then it *is* simple, and a is not a separate symbol but merely a typographical curlicue, and may be omitted, if we decide so. What is essential here is the determination of the grammar of the symbol.

What a name, that is, a simple symbol, refers to in the world is to be considered as a simple object or element in the world. We can take any object whatsoever in our experience and consider it as an element. This simplicity of object is imposed by our language upon the brute 'given' of experience and is thus relative to our language. The grammar of a name is established by an ostensive definition, by actual baptism of a certain bit of our experience by that name. This bit of experience is then an individual or simple element in virtue of the role assigned to it by our language, in the sense that in our language we take it as the end of our definitions, as something that is understood as the meaning of the name without further explanations. We define our symbols by other symbols, but eventually we come to the symbols which we do not define any further because we take them as known directly and indubitably: 'A name cannot be analysed further by any definition. It is a primitive sign' (3.26)—primitive, that is, relative to our language. And the referends of the names are the elements or simple particulars in the world; they are simple, we must stress this, relative to the language, through the determinations of language. There is no sense in speaking of absolute simples. So much for the simple objects or elements in the world, and now to the atomic facts.

Atomic facts are the facts described by atomic propositions. An atomic proposition 'consists of names. It is a connexion, a concatenation of names' (4.22), and contains no other constituents except names. And the concatenations of the elements in the world, corresponding to the concatenations of the names in atomic propositions, are the atomic facts. Atomic facts are thus also determined through language. There is no sense in speaking of absolute atomic facts without reference to language.

It is quite obvious that our colloquial language is not the last word in dealing with experience. Here our discussion and analysis starts with the vague concepts already existent in our language; we start 'somewhere in the middle' and are slowly proceeding from the heritage of the past. Our inherited symbolism may be vague and confused, and we must proceed to clarify and modify it to suit our enlarging experience. It is doubtful if we actually use atomic propositions in our colloquial language. The usual grammatical forms of our language suggest more than atomic propositions should contain. For example, 'this is red' suggests modality by its verb, and is not specific as to the shade of red. It is not a precise and irreducible proposition even in our colloquial language, and thus it does not stand for an atomic fact. But these difficulties of producing genuine simple names and atomic propositions are now, in the light of the preceding discussion, merely practical difficulties, and we know now what to do to overcome them: we are to look for precision in determination of our grammar; our criteria are not to be found, but must be decided upon. And this is the business of the philosophers. A philosopher must clarify the rules of language; he must step in whenever the rules are unclear, confused, or conflicting, and help to extricate us from these difficulties. He has to do this not by any appeals to facts or truths of experience, but by unraveling the grammatical confusions of our language and by suggesting more adequate rules. If we cannot find genuine names and atomic propositions in our language, then either the grammar of our language is too vague and amorphous or we do not use it carefully enough. The cure is to be sought in improving the grammar and in using it more accurately.

1.42   Before ending my discussion of objects and atomic facts I will insert a brief section on Wittgenstein's view that 'Atomic facts are independent of one another' (2.061). This has a bearing on Wittgenstein's theory of propositions as truth functions of atomic propositions, and on his theory of inference, subjects dealt with in his Chaps. 4, 5, and 6, and which I treat primarily in my Chap. 3. Here I will discuss them only insofar as they are connected with my discussion of atomic facts.

A name—a simple symbol—has no parts which are symbols; within the context of our language it is taken as having no structure. And therefore it is logically independent of any other name; we cannot deduce anything about any other name from the grammar of a name. Names cannot contradict one another, and a complete obliteration of any one of them would not logically affect the rest. The connection between names when they occur in propositions is logically accidental or external; the grammar of the name is not changed when the name is used in different propositions. Of course, this grammar can be established only in a context of language; we could not have a completely isolated simple symbol all by itself without language. Even simple symbols can emerge only out of complex experiences. But nevertheless the simples are logically independent of each other in the sense of being undeducible one from another. The simple objects or elements of our experience, being determined by names are, consequently, also logically independent of each other. Our knowledge of an element does not logically lead to knowledge of any other element or any atomic fact. In the world of interrelated elements any of the elements may be annihilated without affecting any of the others, because their connection is logically external or accidental. Here again we must admit that we could not have a completely isolated element, because all experience is relational. If our experience were one shade of red, we could have no experience of this shade of red, since we could have no organized world at all. An element if it is to be in the world has to stand in some (external) relation to some other elements; it must be a constituent of an atomic fact. This is a 'form of dependence', but it is not logical dependence in the sense of deducibility of one element from other elements: 'The thing is independent, in so far as it can occur in all *possible* circumstances, but this form of independence is a form of connexion with the atomic fact, a form of dependence' (2.0122).

An atomic proposition is 'a concatenation of names . . . in immediate combination' (4.22, 4.221). And, as names are logically independent of each other, their concatenations in atomic propositions are logically external or accidental to the names. Moreover, no complex part of an atomic proposition can be taken as a unit constituent of an atomic proposition, because such a unit would itself be an atomic proposition, and the first atomic proposition would contain another atomic proposition as a part, which is contrary to the definition of an atomic proposition. Thus, from an atomic proposition nothing can be deduced except itself and the names which compose it: 'From an elementary [atomic] proposition no other can be inferred' (5.134), and atomic propositions are thus logically independent of each other. Now, as the atomic facts are defined as the facts described by atomic propositions, we come to the important conclusion that 'atomic facts are independent of one another' (2.061), that is, that 'from the existence or non-existence of an atomic fact we cannot infer the existence or non-existence of another' (2.062). 'In no way can an inference be made from the existence of one state of affairs to the existence of another entirely different from it' (5.135).

From the independence of atomic propositions one from another, and the consequent independence of atomic facts one from another, it follows that in order to know all the atomic facts in the world we must know all the true atomic propositions. The possession of all the true atomic propositions is a *necessary* condition for knowing the world completely. But Wittgenstein goes even farther and says that it is also a *sufficient* condition: 'The specification of all true elementary propositions describes the world *completely*' (4.26) (the italics are mine). And this sufficiency of atomic propositions for a complete description of the world implies that molecular propositions, that is, propositions which are not atomic, do not describe anything in the world over and above what can be described by the atomic propositions; in terms of facts this means that there are in the world no molecular facts, that 'the totality of existent atomic facts is the world' (2.04).

This discussion of atomic propositions and facts has bearing upon Wittgenstein's theory of propositions as truth functions of atomic propositions and upon his theory of inference or deduction. I will deal in my last chapter with more technical aspects of these two subjects, but I wish to discuss them briefly here insofar as they are connected with my presentation of atomic propositions and facts.

Atomic propositions are the original and the only material of our knowledge of the world. They do not refer to any other propositions but refer directly to the world and are the material out of which all the other (the molecular) propositions are built by means of artificial syntax: 'the introduction of the elementary [atomic] propositions is fundamental for the comprehension of the other kinds of propositions' (4.411). Molecular propositions are truth functions of atomic propositions (5); they are the expressions 'of agreement and disagreement with the truth-possibilities of the elementary [atomic] propositions' (4.4); they are 'results of truth-operations on the elementary propositions' (5.3), where 'the truth operation is the way in which a truth-function arises from elementary propositions' (5.3). Thus we build molecular propositions out of atomic propositions without adding any new subject matter of our knowledge of the world. Molecular propositions are merely symbolic devices for combining atomic propositions according to the rules of our language, and are needed merely as compensation for our lack of more complete knowledge of the world. By means of molecular propositions we can speak of truth possibilities of atomic propositions where we lack knowledge of their actual truth values. For example, when we have the proposition $p \vee q$, where p and q are atomic, that means that we do not know whether p and q are true or false, but we hold that out of the four possibilities of their joint assertion, namely, $p \cdot q$, $\sim p \cdot q$, $p \cdot \sim q$, and $\sim p \cdot \sim q$, one of the first three is true while the fourth one is false. However, even if $p \vee q$ is true, *only one* of the three admitted possibilities can be actually true, but unfortunately we do not know which one that is. The proposition $p \vee q$ expresses a wider range of possibilities than is actually the case in the world; this range includes the actual case, but it also includes more as a safety measure, because our knowledge of the circumstances here is not complete. The proposition $p \vee q$ is a confession that our knowledge of the circumstances is inadequate to pronounce directly on the truth values of p and q; $p \vee q$ provides for a possible range of facts which is wider than the actual because we do not know what the actual case is. This is somewhat analogous to the case of our expecting someone to come to San Francisco from New York by railroad; we know, let us say, that he may come by one of three trains—from north, south, or east, but not from west; but we do not know exactly by which of the three he is actually coming. If we knew, we would not need such a proposition as 'He is coming either from north, or south, or east, but not west'; we could simply state, say, 'He is coming from the north'. As Bradley said, 'If I saw further I should be simpler'.

All inference is for Wittgenstein formal inference or deduction: 'All inference takes place a priori' (5.133). Induction is not inference but a guess: 'The process of induction . . . has no logical foundation but only a psychological one' (6.363, 6.3631). Inference consists of analysis of a complex symbol constructed according to the rules of our symbolism into its parts. Inference is thus nothing but unfolding of the rules of our complex symbols; it proceeds within the grammar of our language, is independent of facts, and does not lead to any knowledge of facts: 'Only that which we ourselves construct can we foresee' (5.556). Only the rules embodied in our symbols can justify inferences. We can say that we correctly infer one symbol from another because we proceed according to this or that rule, but not because this or that is the case. The rules are arbitrary, but what follows from them is not arbitrary but necessary; and that is the only kind of necessity that we can have: 'In our notation there is indeed something arbitrary, but *this* is not arbitrary, namely that *if* we have determined anything arbitrarily, then something else *must* be the case' (3.342).

Inference, on this interpretation, is not restricted to propositions, but is possible with any complex symbols; Wittgenstein seems to disagree with this, and I will return to this question later on. Here, we are interested only in propositional inference in connection with our discussion of propositions. Propositional inference is restricted to molecular propositions. Atomic propositions, being logically independent of one another, can lead to no inference except to their constituent names: 'From an elementary [atomic] proposition no other can be inferred' (5.134). But molecular propositions, being complexes constructed out of atomic propositions as units, allow of inference to other propositions, either atomic or molecular. Our propositional analysis of inference will consist merely of unfolding the rules of grammar used in the construction of molecular propositions. Inference is purely analytical and proceeds in the realm of our conceptual determinations.

1.43 In Wittgenstein's article in *The Aristotelian Society Supplementary* (Vol. IX, 1929), he makes an astounding exception to the logical independence of atomic propositions from one another by introducing a notion of 'exclusion'. He says: 'The mutual exclusion of unanalysable statements of degree contradicts an opinion which was published by me several years ago and which necessitated that atomic propositions could not exclude one another. I here deliberately say "exclude" and not "contradict", for there is a difference between these two notions, and atomic propositions although they cannot contradict, may exclude one another'. Thus if *p* be 'this is red' and *q* be 'this is blue', then *p* and *q* logically exclude the possibility of their joint assertion, and are thus not quite independent, according to this last view of Wittgenstein. The truth table for '$p \cdot q$' in this case is no longer as shown in Table 1. Neither is it the table for contradictions (Table 2). But it has to be written as in Table 3. In Table 3 the first line of the normal table for $p \cdot q$ (Table 1) has disappeared entirely because 'it represents an impossible combination'.

TABLE 1

p	q	$p \cdot q$
T	T	T
F	T	F
T	F	F
F	F	F

TABLE 2

p	q	$p . \sim p.$ $q . \sim q$
T	T	F
F	T	F
T	F	F
F	F	F

TABLE 3

p	q	$p \cdot q$
F	T	F
T	F	F
F	F	F

Here we are faced with two alternatives: (a) Abandoning the view on the nature of atomic propositions as logically independent. That would have to be followed by a serious modification, if not a complete abandonment, of Wittgenstein's theory of molecular propositions as truth functions of logically independent atomic propositions, and of his theory of inference. (b) Rejecting his innovation of the possibility of some atomic propositions 'excluding' each other, and of treating such propositions as not atomic. If we accept (b), then the predicament in which we find ourselves when confronted by propositions which 'exclude' each other, as p and q in Wittgenstein's example above, can then be accounted for in either of the following ways: (1) As our failure to recognize that the given proposition is molecular and not atomic within our language, even though it looks superficially atomic; our ordinary language may not be explicit enough for immediate recognition of the complexity involved: 'The silent adjustments to understand colloquial language are enormously complicated' (4.002). Or (2) as due to the grammar of our language being confused; there may be no clear-cut rules for determination of simple terms and atomic propositions. As I have already pointed out, this is the case with the *Tractatus* itself.

My treatment and criticism of the *Tractatus* so far lead me now quite naturally to take the alternative (b). Wittgenstein's mistake here has two sources, which have been already pointed out (pp. 32 ff.). First, Wittgenstein confuses the empirical, and more specifically psychological, 'cannot' with the 'impossibility' of rules. And, secondly, he sometimes confuses in practice the inadequate grammar of our ordinary language in application to experience with the formal requirements of logically ideal language. These confusions are due fundamentally to his failure to separate the grammar of language from its actual use. We cannot learn from the actual phenomena anything about the nature of atomic propositions, simply because that nature is to be determined by our language and not by the phenomena of direct experience. What, however, we can learn from experience in this connection is the pragmatic adequacy in the application of our language. Experience can teach us whether our grammatical determinations will or will not work in practice, but it cannot dictate to us the determinations themselves. Wittgenstein does not take seriously enough the consequences of his own teaching. If atomic propositions are, by definition, logically independent of each other, then they are independent, and cannot exclude each other any more than contradict each other. There is no logical difference between 'exclusion' and 'contradiction' of atomic propositions, contrary to what Wittgenstein says in his article. Atomic propositions can have no relations one to another except relations externally assigned to them by us, when we combine them into molecular propositions. Thus, I propose to maintain the positivistic view, supplemented by a degree of pragmatism, against Wittgenstein's innovations. The only check on our grammatical determinations is purely pragmatic: whether they work or not for the purposes which we ourselves set up.

And if our grammatical rules 'don't work', is not that an indication of some conflict between the grammar of our language and the independent order in reality? Shall we have to admit the possibility of determinate character of reality apart from our grammar? In a way, yes. Wittgenstein admits this in his mysticism. But then reality taken apart from our language is not subject to our rational discourse—'*the limits of my language* mean the limits of my world' (5.6)—and we cannot discuss what is outside these limits. In the world of experience, however, 'a necessity for one thing to happen because another has happened does not exist. There is only *logical* necessity' (6.37). And so the point here is that any determination apart from our grammar is not 'necessary' in our sense. Even if certain features of our sense experience were never changing, their eternal stability would still be to us merely a matter of accidental fact and not 'necessary'. Things in themselves are outside the sphere of discourse—that we have to take seriously.

Symbol and Sign

This chapter on symbol and sign is a continuation of the discussion of the previous chapter on language, but it is narrowed down to the more specific aspects of the subject. It deals mainly with the material of the third chapter of the *Tractatus*, but by no means is confined to it. I group my discussion here primarily around the topics of symbol and sign.

2.1   I find it convenient to preface this discussion by some preliminary remarks on thought and logic, in order to clarify the opening paragraphs of the third chapter of the *Tractatus*.

2.11   Thought is defined as 'the logical picture of the facts' (*Tractatus*, 3) and again as 'the applied, thought [past participle, *gedachte*], propositional sign' (3.5), and as 'the significant proposition' (4). Thought is a propositional sign used according to the rules of our language; it is a symbol or a proposition about something or other in the world, and is not necessarily mental. Plato said, anticipating John Watson, that 'thinking appears to me to be just talking . . . to oneself and in silence' (*Theaetetus*, 190), and that 'thought and speech are the same with this exception that what is called thought is the unuttered conversation' (*Theaetetus*, 263); Wittgenstein very logically goes further than Plato and declares thought and significant language to be one and the same thing, namely, the use of any parts of our experience as sym-

bols for some other parts. Thus, thought is not to be identified
with psychological processes. It is essentially connected with
symbolism, but is not confined to any particular material to
be used in symbolism; images, spatial objects, sounds, marks
on paper, or anything else may be used for our signs, and
they need not be confined to anything mental. The problem
of the duality of thought and the world is simply abolished
on this view.

That a fact is thinkable means that we can make pictures of
it to ourselves, can express it by a proposition of our language.
But what can be known has to be thought, has to be expressible in language; and thus what can be known about the
world is limited by the possibilities of our language, by the
limits of our thought: 'The thought contains the possibility of
the state of affairs which it thinks' (3.02), and 'The totality
of true thoughts is a picture of the world' (3.01). The term
'totality' here is unfortunate and should not have been used.
What Wittgenstein wishes to say, I think, is that our knowledge of the world is confined to the true propositions which
we make describing the world of experience; that there is no
a priori way of knowing the world; and that outside the world
of experience, that is, the world which is describable by atomic
propositions directly referring to it, there is no sense in talking about any other world.

The statement that 'we cannot think anything unlogical,
for otherwise we should have to think unlogically' (3.03)
appears to be a dogmatic rationalistic limitation on our thinking; but it merely means that we cannot speak grammatically
without obeying the rules of grammar, that we can make
sensible propositions only by constructing them according to
the rules of our language. Wittgenstein does not intend to
say that we cannot make factual mistakes, or commit logical
fallacies. It is quite obvious that we can, because we often
do, to our grief. But even in order to make a factual mistake
we must first have a significant proposition whose sense has
been grammatically determined, but does not correspond to

the facts; before we can make a mistake, we must have a properly constructed proposition by means of which we can then make the mistake. And a purely logical fallacy means that we have broken the rules of grammar of our language; it follows then, of course, that we no longer talk correctly, but are merely playing haphazardly with our symbols, talking nonsense. Within the rules of our language we cannot break these rules; and without these rules we are outside the language and therefore no longer talk sense.

Thought is possible only through symbolism, and symbolism requires rules. A thought without the rules of its symbolism is simply not a thought. But any process proceeding according to rules is a logical process; thinking is necessarily logical, or not thinking at all. And this brings us to the problem of Wittgenstein's view on logic.

In my next chapter I will deal with the more technical aspects of Wittgenstein's treatment of logic. Here I will discuss his general view.

2.12 The term 'logic' is used ambiguously in philosophical literature. On the one hand it means, especially in contemporary literature, a symbolic system of signs explicitly formulated on paper; on the other hand it means the subject matter which this explicit system expresses or at least exemplifies, for instance, the fundamental laws of thought (whatever those may be), the universal aspect of the world, the domain of eternal truths, or essences. The distinction has been recognized by, for example, George Boole, for whom logic in the second sense was 'the fundamental laws of those operations by which reasoning is performed', while logic in the first sense was the explicit 'expression of them in the symbolic language'. This distinction is also recognized by B. A. Bernstein when he says that 'the logic of propositions itself must have a general logic, an unsymbolized logic, underlying it' (*Bulletin of the American Mathematical Society*, 1926, p. 712). Wittgenstein's meaning of logic does not quite coincide with either of these.

2.121   To explain his view it would be better, perhaps, not to use the substantive form 'logic' at all. This very form in our colloquial language embodies an erroneous approach to the question. 'Logic' is a substantive, and we are inclined to follow the suggestion of our everyday language and think of logic in a substantival way as *something* in the world, or about the world, or beyond the world, at any rate as *some thing*, be that mental, physical, or metaphysical. Even when we speak of logic as a body of tautologies we may be inclined to take this substantival point of view, and think of logic as a subsistent system of disembodied and yet in some way substantial Platonic forms (I am myself tempted to take that view), or Santayanian essences. Perhaps, to express Wittgenstein's view it would be better to use an adjectival or an adverbial form of expression, and speak of something being *logical,* or done *logically.* 'Logical' or 'logically' is equivalent to 'what formally follows the rules of symbolism', to 'the consistent use of symbols'. Of course, to insist on the verbal distinctions in our everyday language in dealing with the subject which is, according to Wittgenstein, intrinsically incapable of being expressed in any language, would be mere pedantry; and, therefore, while keeping in mind the above remarks, I shall continue to use the more common substantival form and speak of 'logic'.

Wittgenstein's use of the term is still slightly ambiguous, and we may distinguish the wide and the narrow meanings. In the wide sense 'logical' is what follows from the rules of any symbolism—a consistent use of any symbolism whatsoever. In the narrower sense, 'logical' means tautological, in connection with propositions. In this sense logic is restricted to one particular kind of symbolism, namely, propositional, since Wittgenstein's theory of tautology is based on his theory of truth functions of atomic propositions. This second use then depends on the view we take of the nature of atomic propositions; and, on a certain interpretation of Wittgenstein, may even lead us to a metaphysics of the Platonic kind. But, if we agree that the atomicity of a proposition is to be determined arbitrarily (as I contended in Chap. 1) by convention, then this second meaning is but a narrower use of the first. In either case, on my interpretation, logic is concerned with the rules of our symbolism, and not with the objects and facts symbolized; it is merely the consistent use of our symbols. This view seems to be fairly close to the 'heterodox view' as presented by C. I. Lewis in his *Survey of Symbolic Logic* (p. 355).

Logic then means for Wittgenstein a consistent use of symbols or, to use the more ambiguous substantival form of expression, the body of all the possible transformations of our symbols according to the rules of our symbolism. The rules may be arbitrary, and the nature of the signs which we use to express them is arbitrary; but, if we are to talk sense, we must follow the rules. The essence of this view is expressed by Wittgenstein as follows: 'In our notations there is indeed something arbitrary, but *this* is not arbitrary, namely that *if* we have determined anything arbitrarily, then something else *must* be the case' (3.342). Logic deals with rules, and not with the reality to which the symbols may happen to refer; we deal in logic with and within the symbolic rules of our language: 'In logical syntax the meaning of a sign ought never to play a role' (3.33); 'without troubling ourselves about a sense and a meaning, we form the logical propositions out of others by mere *symbolic rules*' (6.126).

2.122 It is essential to see that logic deals only with grammatical determinations and not with the world, that logic is not a science: 'Our fundamental principle is that every question which can be decided at all by logic can be decided off-hand' (5.551), that is, without any appeal to experience. 'And if we get into a situation where we need to answer such a problem by looking at the world, this shows that we are on a fundamentally wrong track' (5.551). 'Theories which make a proposition of logic appear substantial are always false' (6.111); 'the whole philosophy of logic' is contained in the fact that 'it is the characteristic mark of logical propositions that one can perceive in the symbol alone that they are true' (6.113). (I will add that in order to avoid a possible confusion of logical with empirical truth, it would be, perhaps, better if Wittgenstein used here instead of the term 'true' the term 'valid'.) What we 'perceive in the symbol alone' without reference to the symbolized is merely the grammatical determination which changes the given signs into the symbols of our language. Logic does not deal with facts in the world, but is merely the consistent use of signs according to the rules of our symbolism; it deals merely with the formal aspects of our language: 'we are in possession of the right logical conception, if only all is right in our symbolism' (4.1213). Of course, we could not have logic in an absolute vacuum, without any experience in which to use it. But while we need experience in order to use logic, logic does not deal with experience as its subject matter, but only with our ways of handling it: 'The "experience" which we need to understand logic is not that such and such is the case, but that something *is*; but that is *no* experience' (5.552).

In particular, logic is not a theory of the most general properties of the world. The view that logic is a science dealing with abstract and general features is a very common one among logicians. J. N. Keynes holds it, and it has been sometimes shared even by Russell. For example, in his *Introduction to Mathematical Philosophy* (p. 169), Russell says that 'logic is concerned with the real world just as truly as zoology, though with its abstract and general features'. But Wittgenstein decidedly rejects this view: 'The mark of logical propositions is not their general validity' (6.1231). Even the familiar 'laws of thought' are but a few special rules of our colloquial language; for example, the law of contradiction ($p . \sim p$) is merely a rule regulating our use of '$\sim$' or 'not'. Personally, I disagree with Wittgenstein and Russell on this view of the law of contradiction. I am inclined to accept Aristotle's view that the law of contradiction is fundamental and indispensable in all our thinking (*Metaphysics*, 1005^b). That generality or even general validity lacks necessity, and therefore is not a logical property, follows from the fact that there are exhaustive generalities which are obviously not necessary. For example, 'All men in this room are over ten years of age' and, similarly, 'All men are mortal', even if they are true, are not necessary propositions, and are therefore not logical. On the other hand, the necessity may be present in an ungeneralized proposition, as in 'It either rains now or it does not'.

We must also understand that, while logic deals with symbols, it is not concerned with the actual psychological processes which may be going on in our minds when we deal with symbols. Identification of psychology with logic is due to the fallacy of psychologism: we find that in understanding certain logical principles we have to go through certain psychological experiences, and we conclude that the two are one and the same. For logic this coincidence is accidental and irrelevant. Many logicians were guilty of this fallacy; Boole held that logic dealt with 'the nature and constitution of the human mind'. But for Wittgenstein logic 'results from the *essence* of the notation' (3.342), and not from the kind of material out of which the signs of our symbolism may happen to be made. Perhaps psychology may happen to have a special epistemological interest for us, but in a discussion of logic it has no privileged position. To give it a priviliged position is a sheer metaphyscal anthropomorphism. 'Psychology is no nearer related to philosophy, than is any other natural science' (4.1121). The fallacy of psychologism in logic is due to the confusion of the validity of thought with certain logically accidental experiences always associated with correct thinking. A genetic account of logic is entirely irrelevant to the essence of logic.

It may, and often does, happen that our psychological processes do not follow the rules of our language, as when we dream or talk nonsense. Then we do not logically think,

but merely have a psychological experience. The inmates of
the so-called insane asylums are especially prone to do this.
When we are confronted with a person who, as a persistent
Hegelian, uses words of our language with disregard of its
grammar, we realize that there are no sound thoughts in the
noises the man is making, and that any discussion with him is
futile; in the case of a Hegelian we are simply confronted with
the case of a peculiar and highly elaborated madness and not
with any new logic.

Thus, logic is not to be found in the world, and it follows
that we cannot express logic by significant propositions describing it as something factual in the world. From the very
nature of logic as the consistent use of symbols, it follows
that logic itself cannot be significantly symbolized in its turn:
'That which expresses *itself* in language, *we* cannot express by
language' (4.121); rather, a consistent use of symbol *is* logic,
or expresses the logic involved. Thus, a logical statement P
"shows itself" to be logical. A statement Q attempting to say
this about P does not do it any more than statement P does
itself. At the end of any explanation we have to come to something which we cannot explain any further; and logic, being
assumed in any rational discourse whatsoever, cannot be explained in its turn by a discourse but has to be grasped intuitively when it is present. 'The propositions *show* the logical
form of reality' (4.121), but they do not express it as they
express facts. We may explain a specific logical connection
by showing it to be a consequence of some wider logical connection, but we cannot ultimately explain the notion of
logical connection because all explanation will have to involve
it. We find ourselves here in what H. M. Sheffer calls the
'logocentric predicament': 'In order to give an account of logic
we must presuppose and employ logic' (*Isis,* 1926, pp. 226 ff.).
We can, of course, exemplify logic by giving examples of
the consistent use of symbols, but we cannot describe it as
something separate from language. As Sheffer puts it, 'Our
aim should be, not to validate logic, but to make explicit, at

least in part, that which we have assumed to *be* valid' (*Isis*, 1926). 'It now becomes clear why we often feel as though "logical truths" must be *"postulated"* by us. We can in fact postulate them in so far as we can postulate an adequate notation' (6.1223). Logic consists not of symbols or even of the rules of symbolism, but only in following the rules of symbolism; it is the proper *use* of symbols.

In discussing the relation between logic and the world we must avoid making the initial mistake of considering logic as something substantial. Logic and the world should not be considered as having side-by-side separate existences, as if logic were something existing by itself in reality and only externally applied to a world that is somehow unlogical until logic is applied to it. This external theory of logic as something substantial leads to an insuperable barrier between logic and the world, as it does in Plato, and should be avoided by the different initial positing of the problem. The world is more than logical but it is at least logical, in the sense that we cannot have it except as organized through the activity of language; and, as this activity has to proceed according to rules, that is, must be logical, the world also is inevitably logical.

2.123   In his discussion of logic Wittgenstein again occasionally suggests some traces of metaphysical realism. In this he is probably under the influence of the Platonism of Frege and the recurrent Platonism of Russell. Logic occasionally seems to be considered by Wittgenstein as some hidden feature of the structure of reality itself: 'Logic is . . . a reflexion of the world' (6.13); 'The propositions *show* the logical form of reality' (4.121); 'it must show something about the world that certain combinations of symbols . . . are tautologies' (6.124). If we consider tautologies to be based on atomic propositions, and atomic propositions as representing absolute metaphysical atomic facts, then we have our logic based on some metaphysical character of reality. Such passages suggest that there is something hidden or secret in our world, a metaphysical structure which we are endeavoring to bring into light. Wittgenstein in such cases simply confuses the rules of our language with some features of reality. Let us show this by a simple example from geometry.

Wittgenstein says: 'We could present spatially an atomic fact which contradicted the laws of physics, but not . . . the laws of geometry' (3.0321). Wittgenstein seems to say here that geometry is an expression of some hidden fixed features of reality. For argument's sake I will not press the obvious objection to this in the fact that there can be different geometries. Let us take the simple case of the Euclidean cube. My contention is that, when we speak of the geometry of the cube we are not dealing with any body, but only with the rules and definitions of geometry as language and what follows from them. These rules and their logical connections are not in any way drawn out of or extracted from the bodies we call cubes. The 'geometrical cube' is the system of rules of geometrical grammar, a declaration of intent to use certain signs according to certain rules; and the 'real cubes' are the series of perceivable spatial characters which, we assume, are connected according to these rules of the geometrical cube. That there are such recurrent series in the world is a matter for empirical observation the results of which can be only approximate and always uncertain; and, what is important for us here, these observations do not deal with any 'metaphysical cube' in itself, but only with our perceptions, and we do not need to appeal to any hidden eternal characteristics of the 'real cube'. Our mathematics is not a science dealing with metaphysical reality.

Again, just as in my first chapter, I do not wish to stress the suggestions of metaphysics in Wittgenstein; and, I think, we can reinterpret most of the passages in which Wittgenstein speaks of the "logic of the world" in a positivistic and pragmatic spirit without straining them too much. When Wittgenstein speaks of the logical features of the world he simply means the 'internal' or grammatical properties of the language which 'reflect' the world, that is, are applicable in the world; 'the logical form of reality' is after all shown in our propositions, and is nothing but the grammar of our language through which we know the world. No 'ultimate' properties of metaphysical reality are involved in this view.

2.124 I wish to say here a word concerning a moot question of contemporary logical discussions, namely, that of the plurality of logics. On the view here expounded there can be no plurality of logics, because on this view logic is the consistent use of *any* symbolism. All valid symbolisms have this in common—they use their symbols consistently within their own systems of rules; they all employ one and the same logic. The rules of different symbolic systems within our language may be different and arbitrary, but what is the same in all of them and is not arbitrary is the necessity of using their own rules if we are not to talk nonsense. We can have various systems of 'logics' precisely only because they all are constructed consistently, that is, logically; otherwise the systems would not be systems but nonsense. But, we may be asked, how do you explain a system of logic contradictory to yours, one in which, for example, $p \vee \sim p$ is not a tautology but a contradiction? To the man insisting that $p \vee \sim p$ is a contradiction we could give either of the two answers: (1) If he interprets the $p \vee \sim p$ according to the grammar of the *Principia Mathematica* and yet insists that $p \vee \sim p$ is not a tautology, then he is simply mistaken. (2) We can consider $p \vee \sim p$ as a contradiction, but then we shall have to abandon the grammar of *Principia Mathematica,* and give to the signs '$\sim$', 'p', and '$\vee$' new grammatical rules; we simply will have a different symbolic system, with different rules; but the logic remains the same. Various 'alternative logics', for example, of C. I. Lewis or of the Polish logicians, are merely so many various arbitrary symbolic systems within our language.

2.125 I do not attempt to draw a systematic comparison of Wittgenstein's view on logic with those of other philosophers; but in the conclusion of my discussion on logic here I cannot abstain from mentioning a good example of what Wittgenstein does *not* mean by logic, namely, the logic of W. E. Johnson. Johnson seems to combine psychology, metaphysics, science, pragmatic considerations, and logic in any degree he finds convenient at the moment. Thus Johnson says: 'Logic is . . . the analysis and criticism of thought . . . defined as mental activity controlled by a single purpose, the attainment of truth' (*Logic,* Part I, pp. xiii, xvii). Here we have logic (analysis), psychology (mental activity), and pragmatism (purpose). To supplement this generous definition he says, 'No rigid distinction need be drawn between logic and metaphysics, nor . . . between logic and science' (*Logic,* Part I, p. xiii). Thus we add to our list science and metaphysics, and a little later on the same page we add also epistemology and ontology. There are many more meanings of logic for Johnson; but, probably feeling that he might have omitted mentioning some possible meanings, he also speaks sometimes of logic as what 'is to be understood by the logician as such' (*Logic,* Part II, p. 42). That, of course, covers the subject completely. The 'as such', as Frege once remarked, is 'an excellent discovery for writers who are not clear in their statements and do not want to say Yes or No'.

I will postpone until Chap. 3 the more detailed and technical discussion of Wittgenstein's logic.

2.2 Symbol is defined as 'Every part of a proposition which characterizes its sense' (*Tractatus,* 3.31), and sign as 'the part of the symbol perceptible by the senses' (3.32). Sign taken merely as an actual physical occurrence is meaningless, and it acquires meaning or sense (becomes a symbol) only in a certain use: 'In order to recognize the symbol in the sign we must consider the significant use' (3.326). A material mark becomes a symbol only after we assign to it the rules of its usage, its grammar: 'The sign determines a logical form only together with its logical syntactic application' (3.327).

The distinction between sign and symbol is now also made

by Russell and is discussed by him in Appendix C of the second edition of *Principia Mathematica*. Sign is for Russell the class of the factual occurrences, symbol is the vehicle of meaning and sense. Thus Russell says:

When we say 'Socrates occurs in the proposition Socrates is Greek,' we are taking the proposition factually . . . take words and propositions as classes of similar occurrences . . . But when we assert 'Socrates is Greek', the particular occurrences of the words have meaning, and the assertion is made by the particular occurrence of that sentence . . . by means of a particular fact . . . But this particular fact is, so to speak, transparent'; nothing is said about it, but by means of it something is said about something else (*Principia,* Vol. I, pp. 664–65).

Thus Russell now distinguishes the merely factual occurrence of a sign from its use as a vehicle of meaning and sense, that is, as a symbol.

2.21   We can distinguish two main kinds of signs: simple or primitive, and complex or derived. Wittgenstein's usage of terms in this connection is somewhat confusing. Properly speaking, the separation into simple and complex originates with symbols (through their grammar) and belongs to signs only derivatively; unless, of course, we admit that there are absolute metaphysical simples in the world—a view against which I argued at length in Chap. 1. On my interpretation, there is no sense in speaking of the simplicity of signs except as used in the simple symbols; the simplicity of a sign is derivative from the formal simplicity of the corresponding symbol, and is thus determined by the grammar of the symbol, not by the physical nature of the sign itself. However, after the simple signs are determined, the complex signs which are composed of these signs have their complexity independent of the complex symbols in which they are to be used. An existent which by definition has parts is necessarily complex, no matter how used.

Wittgenstein is not very careful in his terminology here. Thus he says: 'The simple signs employed in propositions are called names' (3.202); and 'The name means the object. The object is its meaning' (3.203). In the first quotation 'name' is a sign, in the second a symbol. I think the second quotation is to be taken as the definition of name, because a sign by itself, as a mere physical occurrence without grammatical determination, cannot mean anything. It acquires meaning only when it is used as a symbol: 'Only in the context of a proposition has a name meaning' (3.3). Until given a grammatical determination a sign is not yet even a sign, because it is not yet 'the part of the *symbol* perceptible by the senses', but is merely a bit of sense data not interpreted in any way. Sign is merely a perceptible carrier of the symbol. Without some such carrier the symbol is, of course, impossible, but it is an abuse of his own terminology on Wittgenstein's part to say that a sign has a meaning. Evidently Wittgenstein himself realizes the ambiguity of his usage when he refers to names as 'simple signs' in quotation marks (3.201). Name has a sign-symbol ambiguity, and it is only as a symbol that it has meaning.

2.211   The importance of simple symbols or names lies in their meaning. However, Wittgenstein's use of the term 'meaning' is, unfortunately, also ambiguous. First, 'meaning' is equivalent to the grammatical determination of the name, its connotation, or, to use J. N. Keynes' very descriptive term, the conventional intension of the name; it is Frege's Sinn. We must not identify the meaning of a name in this sense with the purely subjective psychological experiences associated with the name; the latter is what Keynes calls subjective intension, and Frege calls Vorstellung, and Wittgenstein incidentally refers to as 'content'. I shall refer to this first sense of 'meaning' of a name as its grammar. This is the use of meaning in such statements as 'the name means the object' (3.203), and that a name 'alone and independently has a meaning' (3.261), and that 'The meanings of primitive signs can be explained by elucidations' (3.263). Second, by 'meaning' Wittgenstein means the referend (object) of a name whenever the name is used in a proposition. This use corresponds to the denotation, or objective intension, of Keynes, and to the Bedeutung, or indication, of Frege. This is the usage in the statement that 'The object is its [the name's] meaning' (3.203). This second usage seems to be the more common one in Wittgenstein and may be, perhaps, taken as his intended usage. I will then continue to use 'meaning' in the sense of 'indication', except when I shall wish to stress its distinction from the first usage, and then I shall explicitly use the term 'indication'.

The distinction between these two different usages of 'meaning' may be expressed, if we do not press the terms, as that between the adjectival and the demonstrative significances of a name. The fundamental and important distinction here is a case of the wider distinction to be noticed throughout the whole investigation of language, namely, the distinction, on the one hand, between the grammatical determination of the symbols and, on the other hand, the use of these determined symbols to say something significant. The grammar of the name is determined by its indication, and in the last analysis has to be established by some form of what Johnson calls ostensive definition. Wittgenstein says, 'In order to recognize the symbol in the sign we must consider the significant use' (3.326). But after the grammar of a name has been established, it can be referred to in our language without the indicative use. Thus we have words in a dictionary or in grammatical paradigms. Neither a dictionary nor a school grammar text contains significant propositions communicating information about the world; they simply give examples of grammatical rules embodied in the words.

This distinction of two meanings of 'meaning' helps us, incidentally, to interpret some rather puzzling statements in the *Tractatus*, for example, 'only in the context of a proposition has a name meaning' (3.3). By 'meaning' here is to be understood indication, because if the name had not had its grammar before it was used in a proposition, we could not use it in the proposition at all; propositions can 'only be understood when the meanings of these signs are already known' (3.263), that is, when the grammar of the names used is known.

2.212   The detailed and specific investigation of the existing individual names or even of kinds of names in actual languages is not within the purpose of the *Tractatus,* because the *Tractatus* investigates only the general formal prerequisites of all language. How these prerequisites are embodied in the actual living languages is a subject matter of empirical linguistics. Undoubtedly, existing languages are grammatically defective and very complicated, and the task of their analysis would be immense: 'The silent adjustments to understand colloquial language are enormously complicated. . . . From it it is humanly impossible to gather immediately the logic of language' (4.002). The subject-predicate form of it is very apt to mislead us into false analyses of what is simple in our language into the complexity of substantive and adjective; thus, assuming that 'red' and 'patch' are simple elements, the expression 'red patch' seems to make the 'patch' complex, as if 'red' were a part of it. On the other hand, the substantive form may mislead us into taking the words in this form to be simple even if they are elliptic descriptions of complexes, as in 'Socrates'. The distinction between subject and predicate in ordinary language seems to result from the fundamental difference between two kinds of names: substantives standing for particulars, and terms, standing for universals, which characterize particulars. But this distinction does not, according to Wittgenstein, apply to the logical simples of language: 'In the atomic fact objects hang one in another, like the members of a chain' (2.03); and in a proposition 'one name stands for one thing, and another for another thing, and they are connected together. And so the whole, like a living picture, presents the atomic fact' (4.0311). Wittgenstein, of course, does not say that all the names must be of one and the same type or kind. What he says is that their relation in an atomic proposition is symmetrical, in the sense that all the names which occur in an atomic proposition function as the constituents of that proposition in the same way.

It is not clear from the *Tractatus* whether our colloquial languages possess genuine names. On the one hand Wittgenstein says, 'Man possesses the capacity of constructing languages, in which every sense can be expressed, without having an idea how and what each word means' (4.002); that is, we manage somehow to express sense without using genuine names. On the other hand Wittgenstein declares, 'All propositions of our colloquial language are actually, just as they are, logically completely in order' (5.5563). The truth underlying these two seemingly contradictory statements is, I think, that our colloquial language does on the whole meet the formal requirements, but it is vague and confused. It has terms which are used as simples within the given concrete context; and it makes sense, even though not always precise sense, again relative to its own context.

Wittgenstein somewhat neglects, or does not sufficiently stress, the relativity of language to the context: in application the formal requirements are met always relative to the context in which they are used, and by enormous 'silent adjustments' to that context. The names, of course, might be of different types or kinds, as for individuals, qualities, and so on, and it would be a large empirical problem in itself to find out what kinds of names are needed for a language confronted by the data of experience. The determinations of the names would be controlled by purpose, convenience, adequacy, and other practical considerations. The detailed discussion of actual names is, as I have already said, outside the scope of the *Tractatus*.

To sum up our discussion of names we can say that they must possess two characteristics: (1) They must be logically primitive in relation to our language, that is, not further definable in our symbolism; and (2) they must be able to stand as signals for something definite and unique in the world; that is, they must have definite meaning. The important view of the *Tractatus* in connection with names is that our language, in order to be significant, must have simple undefinable terms standing for definite elements in our world: 'The postulate of the possibility of the simple signs is the postulate of the determinateness of the sense' (3.23). With the actual names of living languages the *Tractatus* is not concerned.

2.22   I will now pass to the other large division of symbols, namely the complex symbols. Complex symbols are, of course, constructed out of relatively simple symbols, and they have the following important difference of function as compared with the simple symbols: Simple symbols are signals whose meaning is determined once and for all; their signification in the world has to be learned, and no new signification can be conveyed by them if they are taken in isolation. Complex symbols, on the other hand, are expressions and not mere signals; they are capable of conveying something new, not previously determined once and for all by an ostensive definition. 'The meanings of the simple signs (the words) must be explained to us, if we are to understand them. By means of propositions we explain ourselves. It is essential to propositions, that they can communicate a *new* sense to us. A proposition must communicate a new sense with old words' (4.026, 4.027, 4.03). Complex symbols then are analyzable into names, and they express *sense* and do not merely convey a fixed *meaning*. What sense is I will discuss presently.

2.221   The fundamental and the only indispensable complex symbols in an ideal language would be propositions—more specifically, atomic propositions. A proposition can be called a complete complex symbol because it expresses a definite sense not expressible by the symbols into which it can be analyzed. All other complex symbols may be called, by contrast, incomplete symbols. The term is due to Russell, but in his treatment it is ambiguous. In a sense all symbols, even names, are incomplete because they are the symbols that they are only within the context of the given language. Furthermore, an incomplete symbol is incomplete in two more specific ways not clearly separated by Russell. First, it is incomplete in the sense that it cannot significantly stand alone even in the context of the language, but must be supplemented by some other symbols of a suitable kind before it acquires significance, as $\frac{d}{dx}$, 'the author of *Waverley*', or 'Socrates loves'. Just as in the meaning of names, this sort of incompleteness of incomplete complex symbols is in reference not to their grammar but to their use. Incompleteness in this sense distinguishes the incomplete symbols from propositions but not from names; a name taken alone does not indicate even though it has its grammar: 'only in the context of a proposition has a name meaning' (3.3). Second, an incomplete symbol is incomplete in the sense that it can be analyzed into other symbols without any loss of sense of the proposition in which it occurs; taken as a unit an incomplete symbol is not a constituent of the proposition, in the sense that, when the proposition is completely analyzed into names, the incomplete symbol disappears. This second meaning of incompleteness distinguishes incomplete symbols from names.

The incomplete symbols are not necessary for a perfect language. This is important in Wittgenstein, because for him names and atomic propositions exhaust the indispensable symbols of language. Of course, a language which would abstain from use of incomplete symbols and yet was intended to deal with experience would be intolerably prolix and probably practically useless. Any actual language would have to admit incomplete symbols in the form of general names, classes, descriptions, and so forth. It is important, however, to realize that incomplete symbols do not stand for any entities in reality, but are due entirely to our linguistic devices, which are not theoretically indispensable. A neglect of this may lead us into fruitless and—according to Wittgenstein—meaningless metaphysical speculations. But leaving aside the problem of incomplete complex symbols, we must pass to the fundamental and indispensable complex symbols or propositions.

2.222 What makes propositions, and in particular atomic propositions, of paramount importance in language is the fact that they express sense and that, consequently, they can be either true or false. The formal definition of the sense of a proposition is given as follows: 'The sense of a proposition is its agreement and disagreement with the possibilities of the existence and non-existence of the atomic facts' (4.2). Less formally and perhaps more clearly the same view is expressed in the statement that 'One can say, instead of, This proposition has such and such a sense, This proposition represents such and such a state of affairs' (4.031); and, again, in 'The proposition *shows* its sense . . . how things stand, *if* it is true. And it *says,* that they do so stand' (4.022). The sense of a proposition is its representation of how the things stand, of the state of affairs, from our point of view. There are many other passages in the *Tractatus* illuminating Wittgenstein's view on sense, but the above quotations are sufficient for the present. I will discuss this view of sense under three numbered headings: 2.2221, 2.2222, and 2.2223.

2.2221 First of all, we must observe that the sense of a proposition deals with facts: 'A proposition is the description of a fact' (4.023). This means two things: (a) First, it means that the sense of a proposition deals not merely with objects or their collections in the world, but with complexes of interconnected objects. A proposition is a complex symbol and deals with complexes in the world over and above the elements which go into making up the complexes. 'The proposition is not a mixture of words . . . is articulate' (3.141). Here proposition is contrasted with name. In this view Wittgenstein is opposed to Frege, for whom propositions were but compounded proper names standing for either one of two objects —the true or the false. For Wittgenstein a proposition is a function of names, but it itself is not a name but is essentially a complex symbol. I will deal more in detail with the essential complexity of propositions in my discussion of propositional signs. (b) The second meaning of the statement that 'A proposition is the description of a fact' stresses not the complexity of propositions but their reference to reality. It emphasizes that the sense of a proposition refers to the possible state of affairs in the world of perceptual experience: 'To understand a proposition means to know what is the case' (4.024). It is only by virtue of the fact that propositions refer to the world that they can be either true or false. If propositions were mere sentences not referring to facts, they could be neither true nor false, and all our discourse would be but nonsignificant jabber, even if it were performed according to some syntactic rules. As Aristotle said, 'Yet every sentence is not a proposition; only such are propositions as have in them either truth or falsity' (*De Interpretatione*, 17ᵃ).

To bring out this aspect of the sense of a proposition, we may put it in the form of a question: 'When do we know the sense of a proposition?' The answer is that we know it only when we are able to state the conditions under which we could say whether the proposition is true or false; that is, if we can state the conditions of the possible verification of the proposition: 'in order to be able to say "*p*" is true (or false) I must have determined under what conditions I call "*p*" true, and thereby I determine the sense of the proposition' (*Tractatus*, 4.063). A proposition points through the series of definitions implicit in its vocabulary and structure to the state of affairs in the world. A proposition which does not do so is senseless, and is not really a proposition but merely a concoction of marks: 'If a question can be put at all, then it *can* also be answered' (6.5).

This dependence of the sense of a proposition on possible experience is sometimes expressed by saying that the sense of a proposition lies in its verification, or more accurately in the manner of its possible verification. Wittgenstein himself uses the term 'verification' in the *Tractatus* only once, when he speaks of the truth grounds of molecular propositions (5.101); yet this way of speaking represents his point of view fairly accurately. Only we must not confuse this interpretation of the sense of a proposition (as the manner of its possible verification) with the actual process of the verification of the truth or falsity of the proposition. If we do not know how to verify a proposition, how to go about finding whether the proposition is true or false, we do not know what the proposition says. We do not know its sense. But if we do know how to go about verifying a proposition, then we do know its sense, even if for some practical reason we cannot actually proceed to the verification. The statement of the circumstances under which a proposition is true, is the statement of its sense, and nothing else. The sense of a proposition is determined by mere reflection upon the possible circumstances in the world; the truth is to be discovered by an actual examination of the world and depends on the existence or non-existence of these circumstances.

This way of stating the nature of sense of a proposition makes it clear that sensible propositions are limited to facts. It brings out the distinction between those sensible propositions whose truth or falsehood is difficult to ascertain in practice, and the intrinsically senseless statements which superficially appear to be propositions. In the one case a proposition does refer to facts; its method of verification is known, even if we cannot carry it out actually; in a word, the proposition has sense. In the other case the statement has no sense, contains no instructions for its own verification, does not refer to facts, is thus unverifiable in principle, and is intrinsically a senseless statement and not a proposition at all.

The method of verification of a proposition is not added to the sense of a proposition, but is this sense itself. We do not first understand the sense of a proposition, and then add a method of verification of the proposition; we cannot search for the method of verification as something apart from the sense. Whenever we raise a question about the method of verification of a proposition, it is a sign that we are not clear about the sense of the proposition. By clarifying the sense, we answer the question of the method of verification, the two being one and the same thing. To the question about the method of verification of a proposition, the answer is in the clarification of its sense; and to the question about the sense of a proposition there can be no other answer but the clarification of the proposition itself.

2.2222 The second thing to be observed in connection with the sense of a proposition is that each proposition in a perfect language must have one fixed, definite, and unique sense or method of verification; it must describe one definite fact. This is one of the fundamental principles of positivism: 'There is one and only one complete analysis of the proposition' (3.25). If a proposition has several senses, then we have not one but several propositions misleadingly expressed by the same propositional sign. If the sense of a proposition is not definite, then we have no definite proposition, but only a vague beginning of one, and we ought to proceed to determine the precise sense if we wish to have a full-fledged proposition.

The definiteness of sense is not, of course, absolute but only relative to our language and to the context in which a proposition is used. Thus our colloquial language, which is but a part of thought or language in the wide sense, has its own internal or grammatical limitations beyond which it cannot speak more definitely; it does not have names for the brief particulars of our sense experience, or for all the specific shades of color we can actually distinguish. Such defects can be, at least theoretically, removed, and our colloquial language may be made more adequate to deal with experience, may be made to approach closer to the language of our thought. The limits of language are imposed internally, by its own grammar; the grammar may be, of course, modified, and thus the limits of language may be changed, but at a given state of language we cannot sensibly talk in it about the future limits; when we have different limits in language, we shall have another language, of which at present we can say nothing. But while there is no sense of talking about the ultimate or absolute limits of the refinement of language and, therefore, of the absolute definiteness of sense, we can still speak of the definiteness of sense within the grammatical limitations of the given language and relative to the given context.

On the one hand we may modify the capacity of language, improve it, and thus change the limitations imposed upon definiteness of sense of propositions; on the other hand, within the given language we may have propositions of various degrees of definiteness of sense, in each particular case adequate to the practical requirements of the context in which the proposition is used. But in every concrete case our ideal should be to make the sense of our propositions perfectly definite within the limitations of our language, and relative to the context and the purpose in hand. A fringe of vagueness is, probably, humanly unavoidable in practice, but it must not lead to any ambiguity of the sense if we are to meet the requirements of good language. I say to my friend, 'My pen is on the table'; here the make of the pen, its color, its cost, on what part of the table it lies, in what direction it points, and so on, are all left quite indeterminate in my statement; and yet the sense of my statement is perfectly determinate within the limits of the English language, and relative to the circumstances in which it is made. No ambiguity arises as to the precise sense of this statement within the context in which it is used, and my statement therefore complies with the formal demand for definiteness of sense. When I state the day, the month, and the year of my birth, my statement is regarded by the immigration official as perfectly definite, and he does not raise any questions of the exact minute of my arrival in this world, nor of the meaning of time.

The senses of our propositions are, unfortunately, even in practice not always sufficiently clear and determinate, and we are, therefore, often obliged to proceed to clarify them and make them more determinate. This activity of clarifying and determining the sense of our propositions is, according to Wittgenstein, the philosophical activity: 'The object of philosophy is the logical clarification of thoughts. . . . Philosophy should make clear and delimit sharply the thoughts which otherwise are, as it were, opaque and blurred' (4.112).

2.2223 The third important thing to be observed in connection with the sense of propositions is that the sense is logically independent of the existence of the fact it is about: 'The picture represents what it represents, independently of its truth or falsehood' (2.22). The sense of a proposition deals with 'the possibilities of the existence and non-existence of the atomic facts' and not with the actual facts (4.2). 'To the proposition belongs . . . the possibility of what is projected but not this itself' (3.13). 'One can . . . understand [the proposition] without knowing whether it is true or not' (4.024).

2.22231. This independence follows first of all from the very nature and function of propositions. The proposition is a definite connection of names. Molecular propositions require logical constants in addition to names, but for our purpose here we may restrict ourselves to atomic propositions; and an atomic proposition is 'a connexion, a concatenation, of names' (4.22). And here we must stress the fundamental differences between names and propositions in their natures and functions. A name has a fixed meaning, which must be established by the ostensive definition, that is, by some actual connection between the sign of the name and the object in our experience for which this name is to stand; and the function of the name is to stand as a signal for the object. A proposition, on the other hand, is not established by an actual association of it with the fact which it is to express, but is constructed out of the already established names; and its function is not to stand as a signal for the fact with which we are already acquainted, but to express or represent new facts: 'It is essential to propositions, that they communicate a *new* sense to us . . . with old words' (4.027, 4.03). If the sense of a proposition were dependent upon the fact it represents, then in order to determine the sense we should have to be acquainted with the fact before making the proposition about it; then we could make no propositions about facts with which we as yet were not acquainted, and our language would be reduced to a system of signals denoting specific objects and facts of our old acquaintance.

While the names that go into the making of a proposition are old, with fixed grammar, their connection may be new. Expressed in a different way this means that the words in a proposition are connected by relations external to the names, in the sense that the proposition cannot be deduced merely from the grammar of its names; the names put in a certain arrangement produce a whole with a new character because the relations in which the names are put in the proposition are added to the names arbitrarily. This connection of the names resulting in a definite proposition is, within the limitations of the grammar of language, arbitrary and can be made without experiencing the facts expressed by the proposition. It is quite possible to make connections of names which do not represent the actual facts at all, because there may be no facts in which the objects named by the names occurring in our propositions are connected in the ways in which these names are connected in our propositions. 'In the proposition a state of affairs is, as it were, put together for the sake of experiment' (4.031). 'Everything we can describe at all could also be otherwise' (5.634). There is no contradiction in saying that a proposition has sense, describes a fact, when there is no fact thus described in the world, just as there is no contradiction in saying that a certain rule of the game is valid even if no one ever obeys it, or of having a wish which is never fulfilled. It is thus possible to describe what does not exist; such descriptions do not describe something unreal, but they do describe what is nothing at all.

In this fundamental distinction between names and propositions Wittgenstein is opposed in particular to Frege, for whom propositions were but compounded names (3.143, 5.02). But for Wittgenstein 'states of affairs can be described

but not *named* (3.144). In particular, in connection with
names we cannot speak of truth or falsity. We can say many
things about names—that they are suitable or not, convenient
or otherwise, and so on—but not whether they are true or
false. But the propositions, in contrast to the names, do
possess this duality of truth and falsehood, and that is due to
the fact that they are complex constructs. The possibility of
false propositions offers another argument in support of the
view that the sense of a proposition is independent of facts,
and I pass now to a detailed exposition of that argument.

2.22232 Wittgenstein holds the so-called correspondence
theory of truth. Truth or falsity of the proposition consists in
'the agreement or disagreement of its sense with reality'
(2.222), and thus depends upon the existence or nonexistence
of the facts described by the proposition: 'In order to discover
whether the picture is true or false we must compare it with
reality' (2.223); and 'There is no picture which is a priori
true' (2.225).

If we accept this theory of truth, and yet insist on the dependence of the sense of propositions upon the existence of
the facts they represent, then, in order to account for the
false propositions, we should have to postulate one of the
following: (a) the existence of false or unreal facts corresponding to the false proposition, in the same way as the
true or real facts correspond to the true propositions; or (b)
two different kinds of relation between the propositions and
the facts they represent, one occurring in the case of the true
propositions, the other in the case of the false propositions.

The first alternative is so incredible that it seems to be sufficient merely to state it in order to have it rejected. A 'false
fact' really is an absurdity, even though such a man as
Meinong seems to have considered it in all seriousness, and
even though Russell himself took pains to argue against the
absurdity in his polemic with Joachim. Wittgenstein, of course,
rejects it: 'The propositions "p" and "$\sim p$" have opposite
senses, but to them corresponds one and the same reality'

(4.0621). Facts can be neither true nor false, and "an unreal fact" is a self-contradictory notion. Besides rejecting false facts on the ground of their absurdity, we have to reject them also if we wish to retain the very distinction between truth and falsehood; their admission would completely obliterate the whole difference between the two. But let us pass to the consideration of the second alternative.

The second alternative assumes that there are two different independent relations between propositions and the facts they represent; one holds for true propositions, the other for false propositions. All the facts are considered to be equally real on this alternative, as contrasted with the first one. But this second alternative is also rejected by Wittgenstein:

If one does not observe that propositions have a sense independent of the facts, one can easily believe that true and false are two relations between signs and things signified with equal rights. One could then, for example, say that 'p' signifies in the true way what '~ p' signifies in the false way, etc. Can we not make ourselves understood by means of false propositions as hitherto with true ones, so long as we know that they are meant to be false? No! (4.061, 4.062).

This seems to be quite conclusively a rejection by Wittgenstein of the second alternative. But I will try to make the reasons for this rejection a little clearer, since Russell for a while advocated this second view, and even ascribed it to Wittgenstein.

The truth value of the proposition depends upon the correspondence or noncorrespondence of its sense with the fact it expresses; but it is important to note that on Wittgenstein's view we can understand the proposition without empirical ascertainment of its truth value: 'One can . . . understand it without knowing whether it is true or not' (4.024). Here, however, we must make a distinction: while the understanding of a proposition does not require knowledge of its actual truth value, it always involves the formal *truth claim* of the proposition. *The sense of a proposition always tacitly claims its own truth, never falsehood:* 'The proposition *shows* how things stand, *if* it is true. And it *says,* that they do so stand' (4.022). The truth claim is an intrinsic aspect of the sense of the proposition; a proposition represents the fact and at the same time tacitly claims that this representation is true. We might, perhaps, call this truth claim the logical self-assertion of the proposition. How far this truth claim is justified is another matter; it depends not only on the sense of the proposition with its truth claim, but also on the actual state of affairs. But the sense of the proposition, we repeat, is always put forward as true; otherwise, in order to understand what the proposition says, we would need not only to understand its sense but also to know whether it is to be considered as true or false, and also whether this first consideration in its turn is to be considered as true or false, and so on, indefinitely. Every proposition, even a false one or one 'merely considered' always makes a truth claim in this sense. As W. E. Johnson puts it, 'the consideration of the proposition p is indistinguishable from the consideration of the proposition p as being true' (*Logic,* Part I, p. 52).

Thus the formal truth claim of its own truth is an intrinsic or formal property of the sense of every proposition. On the other hand, the formal claim of its own falsehood is not only not intrinsic to the sense of the proposition, but is logically impossible. That p is false can be said by some other proposition which is about the possible truth values of p, but not by p itself. We cannot make propositions which involve their falsehood in their own sense. The proposition can say only what it says and not the opposite of it, and it always formally says that it is true. The notion of truth is fundamental to the sense of any proposition.

And now we can see more clearly why we should not accept the theory that 'true and false are two relations between signs and things signified with equal rights' (4.061). The truth of the proposition consists in the correspondence be-

tween the sense of the proposition and the fact it represents;
the truth claim of a true proposition is in accord with the
actual state of affairs. The falsehood of the proposition is
not due to another and independent relation of correspondence between the proposition and the fact. It does not consist
in the correspondence between the impossible sense of the
proposition's claiming its own falsehood on one hand, and
the fact on the other. There can be no such correspondence
simply because there can be no such proposition claiming its
own falsity. Falsehood is simply a lack or absence of correspondence, is noncorrespondence between the proposition
and the facts; it is a failure of the truth claim of the proposition to be justified by the state of affairs, and not a justification of the impossible claim.

Of course, the formal definition of the concept of truth as
correspondence between the symbol and what is symbolized
is presupposed in all this discussion. This discussion merely
attempts to bring out that the concept of falsehood is not an
independent concept but is derivative from the concept of
truth. The discussion merely elucidates these concepts. The
true and the false then are not 'two relations . . . with equal
rights'. And thus the second alternative of the double relation
between propositions and facts is to be rejected.

Russell in *The Analysis of Mind*, while discussing truth and
falsehood, ascribes to Wittgenstein this second alternative, so
explicitly rejected in the *Tractatus*. Either Russell misunder-
stood Wittgenstein, or else Wittgenstein in the *Tractatus*
changed his view on the subject. As *The Analysis of Mind*
was written before the English publication of the *Tractatus*,
the second explanation is probably the correct one. Be that as
it may, Russell here contradicts Wittgenstein's view as expressed in the *Tractatus*, and it may be instructive to examine
Russell's view.

Russell says: 'The objective reference of a proposition is
a function . . . of the meanings of its component words. But
. . . differs from the meaning of a word through duality of

truth and falsehood' (*Analysis of Mind,* pp. 271–75). Then
Russell gives his first account of this duality of propositions:
'In order to define the reference of a proposition we have to
take account not only of the objective fact, but also of the
direction of pointing, towards the objective in the case of a
true proposition and away from it in the case of a false one'
(p. 272). This 'pointing' is done by 'the direction of the
belief towards or away from the fact' (p. 272). We notice
that on this view the belief is not incorporated in what
Wittgenstein calls the sense of a proposition, but is an attitude
taken toward the proposition and is external to the proposition; this is in accord with what Russell says in his chapter
on 'Belief'. But, then, to determine the 'pointing' of the belief
we must, on this view, know beforehand whether the proposition is true or false; that is, before we can direct or 'point'
our belief, we must know not only the sense of the proposition but also the actual state of affairs concerned. Russell
himself realizes this consequence of his view, and finds it to
be a 'practical inconvenience' (p. 272); and he proposes
(p. 273) to avoid this 'inconvenience' by adopting 'a slightly
different phraseology'. He proposes now to speak of the
'meaning' of the proposition as itself consisting of the 'pointing' to or away from the actual state of affairs, depending on
whether the proposition is true or false. The 'pointing', we
notice, is now to be done not by the 'belief' external to the
proposition, but by the 'meaning' of the proposition itself. By
this 'phraseological' change, so Russell claims, 'we are able to
speak now of the meaning of the proposition without knowing whether it is true or false', and we 'know the meaning
of a proposition when we know what would make it true and
what would make it false, even if we do not know whether it
is in fact true or false' (p. 273). This is the second account
of his view on the duality of truth and falsehood. Now Russell
can say:

The meaning of a proposition is derivative from the meanings of
its constituent words. Propositions occur in pairs, distinguished

(in simple cases) by the absence or presence of the word 'not'. Two such propositions have the same objective, but opposite meanings: when one is true the other is false, and when one is false the other is true (p. 273).

My criticism of Russell here is that in passing from the first to the second account of his view, Russell has really fundamentally changed the view itself, and not merely adopted 'a slightly different phraseology'. First of all, the 'meaning' of a proposition, that is, what Wittgenstein calls its sense, has in Russell's second account absorbed the 'pointing,' which in the first account was considered to be separate from the proposition. The 'pointing' is now transferred to the proposition itself, and does not any longer belong to the external attitudes to be taken toward it. Second, this 'pointing' or reference of the 'meaning' of the proposition is now determined without prior knowledge of the truth value of the proposition and is derived from the meanings of the words, the meaning here being used in the sense of the grammar of the words, not their indication. This logical independence of the determination of the reference of the sense of the proposition from the actual state of affairs is the most important difference for us in Russell's second view as contrasted with his first. If we try to consider, as Russell proposes, his second view as merely a verbal variant of the first, then Russell's own criticism of his first view must still hold good of the second view as well, and the 'meaning' of the proposition must remain dependent upon a prior acquaintance with the actual state of affairs described by the proposition—exactly the opposite of what Russell claims for his second 'version' (p. 273). On the second view, however, we need no acquaintance with the facts in order to determine the sense of the proposition; the sense is now logically independent of the fact the proposition represents—and that is the view of Wittgenstein.

2.2224   I will now summarize my whole discussion of *sense*. First, the sense of the proposition refers to the fact, the fact which would verify the proposition if it were true. Second, the sense of the proposition must be definite and unambiguous relative to the context of the discourse in which it is used; if we understand the proposition, we know definitely to what fact it refers, and if we proceed to the actual verification of the proposition we know how to recognize that fact and not confuse it with any other facts. Third, the sense of the proposition is independent of the actual state of affairs, of the existence of the fact it describes; the existence or nonexistence of the fact has no effect on the sense of the proposition, but decides only its actual truth value. Let us take for an illustration the proposition 'The pen is on the table'. First of all, this proposition refers to the fact of the pen's being on the table; it describes a possible state of affairs in the world concerning the pen and the table. Second, if we use this proposition correctly, that is, in a proper context, as in a police court, the sense of the proposition is definite and unambiguous; we know then what pen and what table it refers to, and what fact in connection with the pen and the table it describes; we are given definite instructions of how and where to look for the pen, if we wish to look for it; namely, we are to look for the pen on the table, and not to turn away from the table in looking for the pen. The fringe of indeterminateness in our descriptions of the pen, the table, and their actual positions is inevitable, but it must be within the limits permitted by the context in which the proposition is used, and, if it remains within these limits, then the sense of the propositon is quite definite in that context. And, third, we can understand the proposition regardless of whether the pen is actually on the table or not. If I proceed to the actual verification of the proposition, I will go to the table and look for the pen on it. If I find no pen there, the sense of my original proposition does not therewith change; it still refers to the pen on the table, and it still claims that the pen is on the table, even though I now find empirically that there is no pen on the table and that, therefore, the proposition is false. Whether the fact to which the proposition refers exists or does not exist has no effect on the sense of the proposition, but only on its truth value.

Thus, the sense of the proposition refers to the fact, this reference is quite definite relative to the context in which it is used correctly, and it is not affected by the actual state of affairs in the world.

2.23   In my discussion of the complex symbols, or, more accurately, of the complete complex symbols or propositions, I have so far restricted myself to the discussion of their sense. Now I wish to discuss the means used in expressing the sense of propositions, namely, the propositional signs: 'The sign through which we express the thought I call the propositional sign' (3.12). The propositional sign consists of names connected in a definite way: 'The propositional sign consists in the fact that its elements, the words, are combined in it in a definite way' (3.14). And the proposition is the propositional sign in use, that is, the propositional sign interpreted according to the grammar of our language: 'The proposition is the propositional sign in its projective relation to the world' (3.12); 'The proposition is a model of the reality as we think it is' (4.01).

2.231   There is a fundamental difference between the signs used in names or simple symbols and propositional signs. Simple signs can be chosen entirely arbitrarily, and they become symbols through the convention or association of the sign with the object signified by the symbol. Their own character as physical existents is accidental and logically irrelevant to the symbol. A propositional sign is constructed out of simple signs or words, and, insofar as the nature of these signs is irrelevant, its nature is also irrelevant to the proposition in which it is used; that is, the specific physical make-up of the sign is irrelevant to the proposition: 'Accidental are the features which are due to a particular way of producing the propositional sign' (3.34). But—and this is the fundamental characteristic of the propositional signs as contrasted with the simple signs—the propositional signs also possess essential features, which cannot be changed without destroying the propositional signs. These essential features are connected with the very essence of the propositions, namely, with the expressiveness of their sense: 'Essential [features of the propositional sign] are those which alone enable the proposition to express its sense' (3.34). While the physical nature of the simple signs which go into making the propositional sign may be chosen quite arbitrarily, the connection into which they are put in the propositional sign is intimately connected with the sense of the proposition we are to express by this sign. In other words, while the physical nature of the propositional sign is irrelevant to the proposition, its structure, that is, the way in which its elements are put together, is essential: 'The sign of the complex is not arbitrarily resolved in the analysis, in such a way that its resolution would be different in every propositional structure' (3.3442). It is only by virtue of having the particular structure that the sign can be used in the proposition to represent the fact. It is only because the structures of the propositional sign and the fact represented by the proposition have the same form that the proposition can represent the fact: 'That the elements of the picture are combined with one another in a definite way, represents that the things are so combined with one another' (2.15). Thus 'The gramophone record, the musical thought, the score, the waves of sound, all stand to one another in that pictorial internal relation, which holds between language and the world. To all of them the logical structure is common. . . . They are all in a certain sense one' (4.014).

Form is an essential or internal property of propositions and propositional signs. Names do not have to stand in the relations in which they actually stand in a proposition; they remain the same names in other propositions, in other relations; their grammar does not require that they stand in any particular relation, be used in any particular proposition; the form of the proposition is external to the names. But a proposition would not be the proposition it is if the names did not stand in that particular relation to one another in which they do stand in the proposition; the form in which the names are related in the proposition is essential or internal to the proposition: 'As the description of an object describes it by its external properties so propositions describe reality by its internal properties' (4.023), that is, by copying the form of the facts. 'The picture has the logical form of representation in common with what it pictures' (2.2).

Thus, we cannot entirely arbitrarily assign a propositional sign to the proposition because the sign must have the structure of the special form required by the proposition, no matter of what material the sign is made. If this were not the case, then the proposition would not represent the fact, but would merely denote it as a signal; and, while we often do use certain signals, in codes, shorthand, and so on, to denote the kind of facts with which we are already familiar, a proposition is essentially more than a signal, because it can be used to convey new information, to express new sense: 'It is essential to propositions, that they can communicate a *new* sense to us' (4.027). This expressiveness of the proposition depends upon its form: a symbol which can express something must have at least form in common with that something. And the propositional sign used in expressing the proposition must have a structure of the same form as the proposition: 'In order to be a picture a fact [a propositional sign] must have something in common with what it pictures. In the picture and the pictured there must be something identical in order that the one can be a picture of the other at all. What the picture must have in common with reality in order to be able to represent it . . . is its form of representation' (2.16, 2.161, 2.17).

2.232   The form of a proposition is what is common both to the structure of the fact represented by the proposition and to the structure of the propositional sign by which the proposition is expressed; but by itself it is but an abstraction and does not exist apart from its instances in particular facts, apart from the content in which it is embodied. As Aristotle said, 'The "form" means the "such", and is not a "this"—a definite thing' (*Metaphysics*, 1033^{b}20).

2.2321 Wittgenstein distinguishes structure from form. The distinction is not clear but seems to be something like that between relation and relational property in G. E. Moore. Form, it seems, is the possibility of the general concept of structure, and structure an instance of the form embodied in a concrete case: 'The way in which objects hang together in the atomic fact is the structure of the atomic fact. The form is the possibility of the structure' (2.032, 2.033). The structure of a fact is a property of that fact inseparable from the fact; form is an abstraction from the structure of the fact in which it is found, and thus it can be present in the propositional sign as well as in the fact which the proposition represents. It is only by virtue of the universality of form that a proposition can express a fact numerically distinct from the propositional sign used in the proposition. However, the distinction between the structure and the form is not clear, and I will therefore not attempt to use the two terms in clearly distinct ways. Consequently, as far as the form is concerned I will not in my discussion always make the distinction between the form of the propositional sign and the form of the proposition.

Wittgenstein also distinguishes between form and logical form; the difference between the two seems to lie in the degree of abstractness or purity. There seem to be spatial forms, colored forms, and so on: 'The picture can represent every reality whose form it has. The spatial picture, everything spatial, the coloured, everything coloured, etc.' (2.171). But there are also logical forms of language which are involved in every special form as well: 'What every picture, of whatever form, must have in common with reality in order to be able to represent it at all . . . is the logical form, that is, the form of reality' (2.18). The logical form is, then, what is completely separate from the nature of the material the language uses for its propositional signs, something that can be present in every material in the world. In addition to logical form the picture may have other features in common with the pictured, for example, both may be spatial; but the material of the picture may also differ from that of the fact pictured, as when the picture is in sound and the fact it depicts is spatial, and then the picture and the fact have only the form in common, merely the expressibility of one through the other, apart from any qualitative similarity in the materials of both. Logical form is essential to the proposition, whereas the other forms are merely accidental: 'A proposition possesses essential and accidental features. Accidental are the features which are due to a particular way of producing the propositional sign. Essential are those which alone enable the proposition to express its sense . . . that which is common to all propositions which can express the same sense' (3.34, 3.341). For example, a Chinese man expresses a proposition orally in Chinese; another Chinese puts it into Chinese written ideograms; then a Chinese-American translates the proposition into written English; then a technician puts it into the medium of Braille; a blind person reads the proposition by touch and understands it. The sense has passed through a series of signs, each one constructed out of different materials; what is common to all of them is the logical form of the proposition. Similarly, communication might be established between, say, Martians and ourselves by radio, even if Martians' sense experiences are different from ours.

2.2322   Although we can give merely a formal definition of form of propositions as that which is common to two facts, one of which can serve to represent the other, it is impossible to tell in significant propositions what the logical form is. Form is ultimately inexpressible and is a part of what Wittgenstein calls the 'mystic', of which I shall speak in Chap. 4:

Propositions can represent the whole reality, but they cannot represent what they must have in common with reality in order to be able to represent it—the logical form. To be able to represent the logical form, we should have to be able to put ourselves with the propositions outside . . . the world. . . . That which expresses *itself* in language, *we* cannot express by language. The propositions *show* the logical form of reality. They exhibit it (4.12, 4.121).

Ultimately form must be grasped by direct intuitional insight. For example, we can never express what a symmetrical relation is, but we must simply produce it in some examples.

Russell in the Introduction to the *Tractatus* expresses a hesitation in accepting this inexpressibility of form on the ground that Wittgenstein, after all, does manage to say a great deal about it; and Russell suggests a hierarchy of languages as a way out of this difficulty. Russell, however, misses the point, because in the *Tractatus* Wittgenstein has in mind not any one particular symbolic system within the setting of another and larger one, but the fundamental principles of all possible symbolism; and in our discourse we cannot put ourselves entirely outside all symbolism, simply because that would put us outside all discourse. And as to Russell's uneasiness about the fact that Wittgenstein, after all, did manage to convey something that cannot be said, Wittgenstein would probably say that it was due to Russell's confusion between 'to say' and 'to show', that is, between significant propositions about facts and a displaying of the internal forms of language. The statements of the *Tractatus* are not propositions about the facts in the world, but are merely clarifications of the formal features of language itself. The *Tractatus* tries to elucidate the fundamental and universal formal features of all possible symbolism, but it cannot teach them to us any more than school grammar books can teach us the fundamental principles underlying our mother tongue. The *Tractatus* makes us conscious of the fundamental features internal to all language: 'My propositions are elucidatory in this way: he who understands me finally recognizes them as senseless, when he has climbed out through them, on them, over them. (He must so to speak throw away the ladder, after he has climbed up on it). He must surmount these propositions; then he sees the world rightly' (6.54).

2.2323 Practical aids to grasping the forms of our language can be, of course, suggested. We might take the propositions of our language and shear them of as many unessential features as we can. What will be left will be, probably, as close to the embodiment of the forms of our language as we could get at. This method is as old as Aristotle. Wittgenstein seems to have this method in mind when he says:

> If we change a constituent part of a proposition into a variable, there is a class of propositions which are all the values of the resulting variable proposition. This class in general still depends on what, by arbitrary agreement, we mean by parts of that proposition. But if we change all those signs, whose meaning was arbitrarily determined, into variables, there always remains such a class. But this is now no longer dependent on any agreement; it depends only on the nature of the proposition. It corresponds to a logical form, to a logical prototype (3.315).

(Incidentally, this passage also points out that the sense of a proposition is not completely given by its form alone but also depends upon the meanings assigned to the terms occurring in the proposition.) Russell has often described this method of obtaining the forms of propositions; for example, 'The "form" of a proposition is that, in it, that remains unchanged when every constituent of the proposition is replaced by another' (*Introduction to Mathematical Philosophy*, p. 199). And Wittgenstein in his article in 1929, 'Some Remarks on Logical Form', follows Russell's method: 'We get the picture of the pure form if we abstract from the meaning of the single words, or symbols (so far as they have independent meanings). That is to say, if we substitute variables for the constants of the proposition' (*Aristotelian Society Proceedings*, Vol. IX, p. 162). Our colloquial language is, however, according to Wittgenstein, misleading as to the logical forms involved, and from it we can immediately draw but very vague conclusions concerning these forms: 'From it it is humanly impossible to gather immediately the logic of language. Language disguises the thought; so that from the external form of the clothes one cannot infer the form of the thought they clothe, because the external form of the clothes is constructed with quite another object than to let the form of the body be recognized' (*Tractatus*, 4.002). (On this point, however, Wittgenstein seems to contradict himself in 5.5563).

The study of the forms of atomic propositions has hardly even begun, according to Wittgenstein's article 'Some Remarks on Logical Form'. And in the *Tractatus*, Wittgenstein has very little to say explicitly about even the most abstract and general characteristics of the forms of atomic propositions. As far as I can ascertain, the *Tractatus* makes explicit references to only two fundamental characteristics of the pure or logical form of propositions: multiplicity and order.

Concerning multiplicity he says: 'In the proposition there must be exactly as many things distinguishable as there are in the state of affairs, which it represents. They must both possess the same logical (mathematical) multiplicity' (4.04). And, later on, in his article, 'Some Remarks on Logical Form', Wittgenstein says: 'And here I wish to make my first definite remark on the logical analysis of actual phenomena: it is this, that for their representation numbers (rational and irrational) must enter into the structure of the atomic propositions themselves'. This requirement of multiplicity in the essence of our propositions is obvious sometimes even in our colloquial language. Whenever we wish to express a fact about two things, say, that A loves B, or that the pen is on the table, we use at least two terms in the proposition. Of course, we can merely name the fact containing two things; but such a name would not convey the needed information by itself, without being explained by a proposition with two terms. If we wish to express and not merely denote a fact constituted by two objects, we must also have in our proposition two terms; if we have a fact with three objects, we need a proposition with three terms, and so on. Number is an essential factor in the sense of our propositions.

The second characteristic of pure form in propositions is order: 'The propositional sign consists in the fact that its elements, the words, are combined in it in a definite way' (3.14); 'That the elements of the picture are combined with one another in a definite way, represents that the things are so combined with one another. This connexion of the elements of the picture is called its structure, and the possibility of this structure is called the form of representation of the picture' (2.15). A mere aggregate of terms of certain multiplicity does not yet possess form sufficient to make a propositional sign out of it; there must be also an order added to the multiplicity: 'The proposition is not a mixture of words. . . . The proposition is articulate. Only facts can express a sense, a class of names cannot' (3.141, 3.142). The order or arrangement of terms is essential to the proposition: 'The sign of the complex is not arbitrarily resolved in the analysis' (3.3442).

Thus, a proposition copies the form of the fact by denoting each constituent of the fact by the respective constituents of the propositional sign, and by arranging these in the same order or pattern of relationship as exists in the fact: 'One name stands for one thing, and another for another thing, and they are connected together. And so the whole, like a living picture, presents the atomic fact' (4.0311).

2.2324 The characteristics of pure form of the proposition, namely, the multiplicity and the order, are not themselves constituents of the propositional sign, as the names are: 'This mathematical multiplicity naturally cannot in its turn be represented. One cannot get outside it in the representation' (4.041); and 'We must not say, "The complex sign 'aRb' says 'a stands in relation R to b'"; but we must say, "That 'a' stands in a certain relation to 'b' says *that aRb*"' (3.1432). The second quotation, perhaps, needs a little elucidation. If 'a' means a, and 'b' means b, and the relation we establish between '*a*' and '*b*' by writing '*aRb*' means *R*, then the fact that '*a*' stands in this relation to '*b*' in our propositional sign, when used in the proposition, says that *aRb* is the case. In an ideal symbolism the sign 'R' should not appear at all, just as *R* does not appear as a constituent of the fact *aRb*; instead of writing 'R' we should simply order '*a*' and '*b*' in the way which directly reproduces the ordering of *a* and *b* in the corresponding fact. According to Wittgenstein, an atomic fact, and consequently the proposition representing it properly, are constructed out of the corresponding constituents without any special connecting constituents: 'In the atomic fact objects hang one in another, like the members of a chain. . . . The way in which the objects hang together . . . is the structure of the atomic fact' (2.03, 2.032), and 'That the elements of the picture are combined with one another in a definite way, represents that the things are so combined with one another. This connexion of the elements of the picture is called its structure' (2.15). Thus if we use as names in our propositional sign some spatial things, then 'The mutual spatial position of these things then expresses the sense of the proposition' (3.1431), and we do not require another thing to designate the relationship between the things.

In a properly constructed symbolism, that is, in a symbolism without the irrelevancies as well as explicit and implicit abbreviations of our colloquial language, the formal characteristics should not appear mentioned by special constituents of the signs. In our colloquial language the formal aspects of our propositions, that is, number and order, are often designated by special terms; and it does appear then as if these formal aspects of the proposition were also something substantial. But that is a defect of the colloquial language due to its use of artificial syntactic rules which refer elliptically to the form of the proposition by means of special signs, instead of reproducing the needed form through the structure of the propositional signs themselves. In a perfect language we should have no constituents in the propositional sign standing for the form of the proposition: 'My fundamental thought is that . . . the *logic* of the facts cannot be represented' (4.0312).

2.233   In concluding my discussion of the propositional signs and propositions, I wish to repeat two important points. First, a propositional sign is not a proposition until it is used as a proposition in the context of our language: 'The proposition is the propositional sign in its projective relation to the world' (3.12). In other words, we can have a proposition only in use. The propositional sign must be so constructed as to embody the form of the proposition, must be fit to be used as an instrument of expression of the proposition, but it becomes such an instrument only when actually used. Second, a proposition is not given merely by its form, but by the form plus the meanings assigned to the terms used in it as names. The same form may be possessed by different propositions, as well as by meaningless sentences. It is essential to the sense of the proposition that the terms used in the sentence be meaningful terms, that is, names: 'Every possible proposition is legitimately constructed, and if it has no sense this can only be because we have given no *meaning* to some of its constituent parts' (5.4733). To have a proposition there must be names; these names must be put together in a propositional sign of the required form; and, finally, this sign must be used or interpreted.

2.3   In closing this chapter I wish to emphasize the paramount importance of good symbolism. Symbolism arises in response to the needs of practical dealing with experience; later on it becomes also an instrument of more refined and even purely theoretical intellectual life. Unfortunately, the inertia of tradition often retains the earlier and cruder symbolism at times when this symbolism becomes inadequate to the more complex conditions of life; and thus the earlier symbolism becomes an obstruction to the development of intellectual life. Symbolism springs out of some need of life, and is an indispensable instrument in organizing the flux of the brute 'given' of experience; without it we could have no world, no knowledge, no experience outside of aesthetic impressions. But once fixed, the symbolism may become a drag on further development of this organizing process, and then a bar to the growth of intellectual activity. Some aspects of symbolism fixed on one level of development may become fetters if retained on higher levels reached by other parts or aspects of symbolism. Then a need may arise for a revision, perhaps even a revolution, in symbolism. Our life is shot through with symbolism, and the defects of our symbolism may profoundly affect our life. The present-day difficulties of readjusting our society to changing economic and technical conditions are probably due largely to the fact that we still think through languages fundamentally unchanged since the periods of primitive rural economy. Here we may take heed of some remarks by Whitehead:

It is the first step in sociological wisdom to recognize that the major advances in civilization are processes which all but wreck the societies in which they occur . . . Those societies which cannot combine reverence to their symbols with freedom of revision must ultimately decay either from anarchy, or from the slow atrophy of life stifled by useless shadows (*Symbolism,* p. 88).

As an example of adverse influence of obsolete symbolism in a more academic sphere we may point to the traditional subject-predicate form of the Western languages. What is but an accidental and parochial characteristic of a few languages has been taken by philosophers as a fundamental characteristic of reality. Criticisms by such men as Russell have made this adverse influence of the traditional forms of European languages on logic and philosophy a commonplace in contemporary philosophic literature. But it is difficult to shake off the influence of tradition; and Ramsey, one of Russell's own disciples, finds Russell himself likewise a victim of influence of colloquial language, namely, in his theory of universals and particulars. Again, Russell's and Johnson's lengthy and subtle logical discussions are sometimes amazingly intermingled with such parochial and irrelevant linguistic characteristics as the logically anarchistic English articles 'a' and 'the', making the logical problems under discussion complicated and obscure by confusing them with sheer historical accidents of the English language. But perhaps in reforming our symbolism, we have to proceed in the spirit of St. Augustine in his youth, described later in the *Confessions:* 'But wretched youth that I was . . . I entreated chastity of thee and had prayed, "Grant me chastity and continence, but not yet." For I feared that thou should'st hear me too soon'. Perhaps we should not attempt to perfect our language 'too soon' but reform it step by step, piecemeal. Descartes' heroic undertaking of starting with a clear slate of universal doubt is probably humanly impracticable, as Descartes' own attempt showed.

> *. . . Traditional elementary logic, taught in youth, is an almost fatal barrier to clear thinking in later years.*
>
> RUSSELL

Truth Functions of Atomic Propositions

This chapter will deal primarily with Chaps. 4, 5, and 6 of the *Tractatus,* and especially with Wittgenstein's view of molecular propositions as truth functions of atomic propositions in some of its technical aspects. Logic is, for Wittgenstein, closely connected with his theory of propositions as truth functions, and so I will also discuss here some technical features of Wittgenstein's logic, and thus will complete my discussion of his logic.

3.1 Molecular or complex propositions are propositions containing other propositions, and in the last analysis, atomic propositions, as their constituents. More specifically, molecular propositions are truth functions of atomic propositions: 'Propositions are truth-functions of elementary [atomic] propositions' (*Tractatus,* 5); 'A proposition is the expression of agreement and disagreement with the truth-possibilities of the elementary propositions' (4.4), that is, with 'the possibilities of the existence and non-existence of the atomic facts' (4.3). The essence of this view is this: the sense of a molecular proposition is completely determined and exhausted by the statement of the conditions under which the proposition is true or false.

3.11 In colloquial language the forms of molecular propositions are usually marked by special syntactic terms, so-called logical constants, such as 'if', 'and', and 'unless'. Very often, however, these logical constants do not appear explicitly. 'This pen is black' has no explicit conjunction, and yet it can be analyzed into a conjunction of at least two propositions, namely, 'This is a pen, and it is black'; and thus the proposition 'This pen is black' is molecular, relative to our colloquial language, even though at first sight it may not appear to be so. 'The silent adjustments to understand colloquial language are enormously complicated. . . . From it it is humanly impossible to gather immediately the logic of language' (4.002). Nevertheless, some logicians, for example, Russell and Johnson, have tried to gather the possible forms of molecular propositions from observation of colloquial language; Russell, however, wisely abstained from an attempt at exhaustive enumeration of the forms of truth functions on this basis (for example, see his *Introduction to Mathematical Philosophy,* pp. 146 f.). Wittgenstein proposes a convenient systematic method of derivation of all the forms of the truth functions for any number of atomic propositions, and I will now give a short account of this method.

'With regard to the existence of n atomic facts there are $K_n = \sum_{\nu=0}^{n} \binom{n}{\nu}$ possibilities. It is possible for all combinations of atomic facts to exist, and the others not to exist' (4.27); that is, with regard to the truth and falsity of n atomic propositions the number of mutually exclusive ultimate possibilities is equal to the combination of n different things taken 0, 1, 2, $\ldots$, n at a time, that is, equal to 2^n. (Notice that we include in our counting the case where none of the facts in question exists.) We can see this result also from the following simple considerations. An atomic proposition may be either true or false regardless of the truth and falsity of all the other atomic propositions; this follows from the independence of atomic propositions one from another, already discussed in my Chap. 1.

Thus, the number of ultimate truth possibilities of one atomic proposition of the set of n atomic propositions is also 2, independent of the truth possibilities of the other propositions of the set. Hence, the total number of truth possibilities of n atomic propositions is $2 \cdot 2 \cdot 2 \ldots$ to n factors, or 2^n. If, for the sake of illustration, we restrict ourselves to one and then to two atomic propositions, the sets of their truth possibilities may be presented by Table 4 (*Tractatus*, 4.31), where T stands for 'true' and F stands for 'false'.

TABLE 4

Truth possibilities of one proposition, p	Truth possibilities of two propositions, p and q	

p
T
F

p	q
T	T
F	T
T	F
F	F

'With regard to the agreement and disagreement of a proposition with the truth-possibilities of n elementary [atomic] propositions [which are its components] there are $\sum_{\varkappa=0}^{K_n}\binom{K_n}{\kappa}$ $= L_n$ possibilities' (4.42). That is, out of the set of 2^n truth possibilities of n atomic propositions, we may pick out any subset (for example, FT on the second line of Table 4) and agree or disagree with it, and at the same time independently agree or disagree with any of the remaining complementary subsets. This gives us two choices for each subset independently of our choices for any other subset and, thus, we have $2 \cdot 2 \cdot 2 \ldots$ to 2^n factors, altogether 2^{2^n}, number of choices of agreement and disagreement with the truth possibilities of n atomic propositions. In other words, for a set of n atomic propositions we can have 2^{2^n} truth functions of them: there are $2^{2^1} = 4$ truth functions of one atomic proposition, $2^{2^2} = 16$ of two, $2^{2^3} = 256$ of three, and so on. The four truth functions of a single atomic proposition may be presented by Table 5. (For convenience I add the corresponding familiar expressions in the notation of *Principia Mathematica*.)

TABLE 5

Truth functions of *one* atomic proposition

		Truth functions of p			
		1	2	3	4
p	Notation of *Principia Mathematica*	$p \lor \sim p$	p	$\sim p$	$p \, . \sim p$
T	Notation of the	T	T	F	F
F	*Tractatus*	T	F	T	F

No. 1 is what Wittgenstein calls a tautology, No. 2 is the proposition itself, No. 3 is the denial of p, and No. 4 is a contradiction. The truth functions of two atomic propositions can be presented by Table 6 (Wittgenstein's table of 5.101 slightly rearranged). Similarly, we could construct tables for truth functions of any given number of atomic propositions.

The advantage of the *T-F* notation is that it embodies the logic of truth functions in a more simple and comprehensive way than do other known notations. It is, for example, simpler than Russell's notation, which needs complicated instructions. Of course, the *T-F* notation also requires instructions, but these turn out to be much simpler than those required by Russell's notation. This is due to the fact that *T-F* notation finds its support in the language most familiar to us, namely, the word language; *T-F* notation is really nothing but a word language used in a systematic and compact way. It simply says something like 'This statement is true, if that statement is true *and* that other statement is false'. The rules of *T-F* notation are not read from something else, but are the very determinations of the syntax of our language. *T-F* notation plays a role here very analogous to that of the figures we draw and the models we make while studying Euclidean geometry. One is tempted to believe that we determine the geometry of, say, a

TABLE 6

Truth functions of two atomic propositions

		Truth functions of p and q

Truth possibilities of p and q / **Truth functions of p and q**

Notation of *Principia Mathematica* →	1	2	3	4	5	6	7	8	9	10	11	12	13	14	15	16
formula	$p \supset p \cdot q \supset q$	$\sim(p \cdot q)$	$q \supset p$	$p \supset q$	$p \lor q$	$\sim q$	$\sim p$	$p \cdot \sim q \cdot \lor \cdot \sim p \cdot q$	$p \equiv q$	p	q	$\sim p \cdot \sim q$	$p \cdot \sim q$	$\sim p \cdot q$	$p \cdot q$	$\sim p \cdot \sim q \cdot \sim(p \cdot q)$

Notation of the *Tractatus* (truth possibilities of p and q):

p	q	1	2	3	4	5	6	7	8	9	10	11	12	13	14	15	16
T	T	T	F	T	T	T	F	F	F	T	T	T	F	F	F	T	F
F	T	T	T	F	T	T	F	T	T	F	F	T	F	F	T	F	F
T	F	T	T	T	F	T	T	F	T	F	T	F	F	T	F	F	F
F	F	T	T	T	T	F	T	T	F	T	F	F	T	F	F	F	F

triangle from the observation of drawings of triangles. But a drawing is only a clear and convenient representation from which we can read off the geometry of a triangle by a very easy process; the rules of the geometry of a triangle were determined before we could read them off any material representation such as a drawing. Drawing a triangle is a very convenient way of studying the rules of our geometry, but it is not the determination of the grammar of a triangle. And so it is with the *T-F* notation. It is but a convenient embodiment of the syntax of the truth functions of our language.

3.12 Wittgenstein offers a uniform method of derivation of all the truth functions of any given set of atomic propositions by application of one fundamental operation upon atomic propositions, and thus he claims to have obtained the general form of all the possible molecular propositions which can be constructed out of atomic propositions. This one general form of all molecular propositions is what is common to all of them, and therefore it contains the logical constant of our language: 'the one logical constant is that which *all* propositions, according to their nature, have in common with one another. That however is the general form of proposition . . . The description of the most general propositional form is the description of the one and only general primitive sign in logic' (5.47, 5.472). This general form is described by the symbol $[\bar{p}, \bar{\xi}, N(\bar{\xi})]$ which 'says nothing else than that every proposition is the result of successive applications of the operation $N'(\bar{\xi})$ to the elementary propositions' (6, 6.001). (The apostrophe after N is probably a misprint.)

The way in which Wittgenstein arrives at this result may be stated briefly as follows.

'All propositions are results of truth-operations on the elementary [atomic] propositions. The truth-operation is the way in which a truth-function arises from elementary propositions' (5.3). Examples of operations are 'denial, logical addition, logical multiplication, etc.' (5.2341).

According to the nature of truth-operations, in the same way as out of elementary propositions arise their truth-functions, from truth-functions arise a new one. Every truth-operation creates from truth-functions of elementary propositions another truth-function of elementary propositions, i.e., a proposition. The result of every truth-operation on the results of truth-operations on elementary propositions is also the result of *one* truth-operation on elementary propositions (5.3).

For the one fundamental truth operation Wittgenstein chooses the extension of one of the interpretations of H. M. Sheffer's 'stroke' operation, namely, the idea of simultaneous rejection ('neither p nor q', or 'not-p and $\sim q$'). Wittgenstein extends Sheffer's stroke operation from the simultaneous rejection of two propositions to the simultaneous rejection of any number, finite or infinite, of given propositions regardless of the way the propositions are given. This use of Sheffer's 'stroke' operation for determining general propositions leads to what at first glance appears to be a rather strange procedure—stating a proposition by denying its components! But the strangeness is due to no more than a clever technical innovation; and no new logical principles are introduced by it. Russell uses Sheffer's 'stroke' but with a different interpretation in the Introduction to the second edition of the *Principia Mathematica*. This idea of rejection may be expressed roughly as 'All the propositions designated by this symbol are false'. In a little more detail, Wittgenstein's view and notation here is as follows: 'Every truth-function is a result of the . . . operation $(---T)$ $(\xi, . . .)$ to elementary [atomic] propositions. This operation denies all the propositions in the righthand bracket and I call it the negation of these propositions' (5.5).

An expression in brackets whose terms are propositions I indicate—if the order of the terms in the bracket is indifferent—by a sign of the form '$\bar{\xi}$'. 'ξ' is a variable whose values are the terms of the expression in brackets, and the line over the variable indicates that it stands for all its values in the bracket. . . . How the de-

scription of the terms of the expression in brackets takes place
is unessential (5.501). Therefore I write instead of '($---T$)
$(\bar{\xi}, \ldots)$', '$N(\bar{\xi})$'. $N(\bar{\xi})$ is the negation of all the values of the
propositional variable ξ (5.502). If ξ has only one value, then
$N(\bar{\xi}) = \sim p$ (not p), if it has two values, then $N(\bar{\xi}) = \sim p . \sim q$
(neither p nor q) (5.51). If the values of ξ are the total values of
a function fx for all values of x, then $N(\bar{\xi}) = \sim (\exists x) . fx$ (5.52).
In the general propositional form, propositions occur in a proposi-
tion only as bases of the truth-operations (5.54).

And this general propositional form may be written as $[\bar{p}, \bar{\xi},$
$N(\bar{\xi})]$ (6), where p stands for all atomic propositions and
'says nothing else than that every proposition is the result of
successive applications of the operation $N'(\bar{\xi})$ to the elementary propositions' (6.001). (As I said earlier, the apostrophe
after N is probably a misprint.)

A remark of minor importance must be inserted here. Since
the truth operation can be repeated any finite number of times,
it may appear that we could construct an indefinite number
of truth functions out of a given set of atomic propositions by
repeated application of the truth operation. But on Wittgenstein's view this is not so, and the number of truth functions
of a given set of n atomic propositions is definitely limited to
2^{2^n}. Of course, we can construct any number of different symbols for the set of the truth functions based upon the given
set of atomic propositions, but these symbols will give us
merely different ways of describing the same set of 2^{2^n} truth
functions, and no more. We can even express the truth functions of n atomic propositions in terms of $n + m$ atomic
propositions, where m is arbitrary; thus we can express the
truth functions of *one* atomic proposition, say p, as $p . q \vee$
$\sim q$, $p . q \vee \sim q . r \vee \sim r$, and so on; and the truth function
of two atomic propositions, say $p . q$, and $p . q . r \vee \sim r$, and
so on; this way of expressing a proposition may sometimes
be more convenient for certain logical manipulations. The
converse, however, does not hold; we cannot express a truth

function of a certain number of atomic propositions as a function of any smaller number of atomic propositions; for example, $p . q$ cannot be expressed as a function of p alone or of q alone. In a word, we can write in many different ways what is essentially one and the same proposition, expressing agreement and disagreement with the same sets of truth possibilities of the given atomic propositions, but the different ways of expressing the same proposition will not give us different propositions: 'The way in which we describe the propositions is not essential' (3.317).

3.13   Two kinds of propositions deserve special mention because they may not appear to be truth functions of atomic propositions, and thus to be exceptions to Wittgenstein's statement that all propositions are truth functions of atomic propositions. These two kinds are: general propositions, and propositions of the type 'A believes p'.

3.131   General propositions are propositions expressed in English by means of the words 'all' and 'some', and in the notation of *Principia Mathematica* by apparent variables. According to Wittgenstein these propositions are, just as any other propositions, truth functions of atomic propositions. Their peculiarity lies merely in the way of the specification of their truth arguments: instead of enumerating them as all the other molecular propositions do, the general propositions describe them by 'giving a function fx, whose values for all values of x are the propositions to be described' or by 'giving a formal law, according to which those propositions are constructed' (5.501).

Thus, general propositions are truth functions expressing agreement and disagreement with the truth possibilities of atomic propositions, just as other molecular propositions do, but they do this in a different and more complicated way. Instead of containing all the names of the objects it is concerned with, the symbol of a general proposition contains only a variable standing for all its values at once. This peculiarity of general propositions is, however, not logically essential to them, because it is a characteristic not of the senses of these propositions, but only of the mode of their expression, and we must remember that 'the way in which we describe the propositions is not essential' (3.317). The same proposition can be expressed (at least theoretically—the practical difficulty may happen to be unsurmountable) either generally or not generally or, using Russell's terminology, either non-elementarily or elementarily. Thus ' "fa" says the same as "$(\exists x) . fx . x = a$" ' (5.47). Therefore they are one and the same proposition, and yet the first expression is elementary, the second not. Just as it is unessential to a proposition whether it is expressed in French or in English, so it is unessential whether it is expressed elementarily or nonelementarily.

To give somewhat more detail, general propositions are dealt with by Wittgenstein as follows: 'If the values of ξ are the total values of a function fx for all values of x, then $N(\bar{\xi}) = \sim (\exists x) . fx$' (5.52). This defines $\sim (\exists x) . fx$. Here $N(\bar{\xi})$ stands for the negation of all the values of fx (where f is constant). If the values of fx are enumerated directly, then $N(\bar{\xi})$ stands simply for the logical product $\sim fx_1 . \sim fx_2 . \sim fx_3 \ldots$, or more compactly, $\Pi(\sim fx)$; if these values are not given by enumeration but by description, $N(\bar{\xi})$ does not stand for $\underset{x}{\Pi}(\sim fx)$ expressed explicitly but is still equivalent to it. Thus, we can write:

(1) $N(\bar{\xi}) \cdot = \cdot \underset{x}{\Pi} (\sim fx) \cdot = \cdot \sim (\exists x) . fx$ Df.

and

(2) $(\exists x) . fx \cdot = \cdot \sim \sim (\exists x) . f(x) \cdot = \cdot \sim \underset{x}{\Pi} (\sim fx) \cdot = \cdot \underset{x}{\Sigma} (fx)$

$\cdot = \cdot fx_1 \sim fx_2 \sim fx_3 \cdots$

If we start in (1) with $\sim fx$ instead of fx, we will get:

(3) $N(\bar{\xi}) \cdot = \cdot \underset{x}{\Pi} (\sim \sim fx) \cdot = \cdot \underset{x}{\Pi} (fx) \cdot = \cdot \sim (\exists x) . \sim fx$

But

(4) $(x) . fx \cdot = \cdot \sim (\exists x) . \sim fx$ Df.

By (3) and (4), we get

(5) $(x) . fx = \underset{x}{\Pi} (fx) \cdot = \cdot fx_1 . fx_2 . fx_3 \cdots$

Thus $(\exists x) . fx$ may be regarded as equivalent to the logical sum of all the values of fx, and $(x) . fx$ as the logical product of all the values of fx. Here we notice, first, that the character of generality comes in not through a direct enumeration of the atomic propositions involved, but through the description of them as the values of fx; and, secondly, that the truth functions involved are the logical sum in one case, and the logical product in the other. The first characteristic distinguishes general propositions from other molecular propositions, but this distinction is not logically essential. The second characteristic brings them into the general schema of truth functions.

General propositions then are not logically of a different kind from molecular propositions, as Russell thought in *Principia Mathematica*. But while general propositions are logically equivalent to the logical sum or logical product of atomic propositions, the practical difference between general propositions and propositions which are actual logical sums or products is very important, because in general propositions $N(\bar{\xi})$ can be extended to cover an infinite number of atomic propositions. For example, take the proposition 'The ball is somewhere in the box'. We cannot express this as a completed logical sum: 'The ball is here in the box, or the ball is here in the box, or . . .'. There is no way of exhausting all the possible positions of the ball in the box by direct enumeration of these positions. Yet it is quite simple to express this by an equivalent general proposition, 'The ball is somewhere in the box'. More obvious cases would be 'All men are mortal', and 'Somebody has stolen my purse'.

To these sketchy remarks on general propositions I wish to add that many expressions which appear to be general propositions are not, strictly speaking, propositions at all. This is particularly the case with scientific laws. These laws are not general propositions, but are merely patterns or models for the formation of propositions: 'All propositions, such as the law of causation, the law of continuity in nature . . . , etc., etc., all these are a priori intuitions of possible forms of the propositions of science' (6.34). For Wittgenstein the laws are not propositions because they are even theoretically unverifiable, once we reject induction as a logical process. For Wittgenstein induction is but a guess, a leap into the dark of the future: 'The events of the future *cannot* be inferred from those of the present' (5.1361). Scientific laws may be convenient or otherwise, may be confirmed or refuted by practice, but they cannot be verified. Science for Wittgenstein is not merely descriptive but is also a forecasting theory; the forecasting, however, is but a guess and has no logical foundation.

3.132   The second kind of propositions which may appear to be exceptions to Wittgenstein's extensional theory of propositions (that is, that all propositions are truth functions) are the propositions of the type 'A believes p', which may be called intensional or attitudinal.

At first sight it appears as if there were also a different way in which one proposition could occur in another. Especially in certain propositional forms of psychology, like 'A thinks, that p is the case', or 'A thinks p', etc. Here it appears superficially as if the proposition p stood to the object A in a kind of relation (5.541).

The essence of the extensional view of propositions as truth functions is this: The sense of a proposition is completely determined by the statement of the conditions under which the proposition is true or false. On this view the psychological subjective element (the 'content', the 'presentation' of Frege), the imagery or the feelings or emotions which may happen to accompany one's understanding of the proposition, are excluded from the sense of the proposition. And it may appear that this view cannot account for the propositions of the type exemplified by 'A believes *p*' because the psychological element, namely, the state of mind of A towards the proposition *p* seems to be an integral part of the whole proposition 'A believes *p*'. A may very well believe *p* to be true when it is actually false, or believe it false when it is actually true. The truth value of 'A believes *p*' seems to be decided by the state of mind of A, and not by the truth value of *p*. Although Wittgenstein rejects the usual intensional interpretation of the proposition 'A believes *p*', he cannot deny that its truth value does not depend on the truth value of the proposition *p* which seems to be its constituent. 'A believes *p*' appears by its form to be a truth function of the proposition *p*, and yet it is not. In order to eliminate this seeming contradiction, Wittgenstein has to show that the apparent form of the 'A believes *p*' is not its real form, and that its real form does not contain the proposition *p* as a constituent; that is, he has to show that 'A believes *p*' is not a truth function of *p*.

Wittgenstein's solution of this problem is stated as follows: 'But it is clear that "A believes that *p*", "A thinks *p*", "A says *p*", are of the form " '*p*' says *p*"; and here we have no co-ordination of a fact and an object, but a co-ordination of facts by means of a co-ordination of their objects' (5.542).

Since Wittgenstein considers that the various intensional propositions he mentions are of the same form, I shall confine myself to only one of them, the simplest: 'A says *p*'. Here then we have a propositional sign 'A believes *p*'. (Usually I refer to 'A believes *p*' simply as a proposition, but, strictly speaking, it is a propositional sign expressing a proposition. However, unless there is a special need of avoiding confusion, I shall continue to refer to it simply as a proposition). By means of 'A says *p*' we express the proposition referring to or (in Wittgenstein's terminology) standing in relation to the possible fact of Mr. A's making the series of sounds '*p*' ('*p*' is always complex). 'The sign through which we express the thought I call the propositional sign. And the proposition is the propositional sign in its projective relation to the world' (3.12). Thus our proposition, expressed by 'A says p', is about Mr. A making certain noises 'p', and *not* about the proposition p. The sign 'p' is not used in 'A says p' to express the proposition p, but is merely a physical occurrence which is a part of the physical sign 'A says p'. (As a part of the sign 'A says p' the last letter is only a physical occurrence; and when I use it standing alone, I put quotation marks around it to indicate that it functions merely as a physical thing, and not as a propositional sign for p). The important point to notice is that we are not dealing here with the proposition p at all. The proposition expressed by 'A says p' is not a truth function of the proposition p. The apparent form of 'A says p' is not its real form, and the real form does not contain the proposition p as a constituent. That is the Wittgenstein point. 'A says p' is an atomic proposition.

In the situation discussed so far the proposition p has turned out to be irrelevant. But the situation would completely change if, instead of making statements about Mr. A's doings, we listened to him saying 'p!' Then we would have to deal not with Mr. A and his noises, but with the proposition p standing in projective relation to some possible state of affairs in the world, very likely quite different from Mr. A and his noises. And, moreover, the proposition p itself may be about some psychological matters. Wittgenstein's theory does not preclude making significant statements about psychological facts. Genuine psychological facts are, perhaps, more difficult to deal with objectively than are many other kinds of facts, such as biological or chemical facts, but there is no reason for making special dispensations for them in the logic of our language. Propositions about them have to be truth functions of atomic propositions about facts in the psychological sphere. 'Mr. A is in a contrite mood *and* Mrs. A is pleased' is a perfectly good truth function of 'Mr. A is in a contrite mood' and 'Mrs. A is pleased'. The difficulties of ascertaining whether Mr. A is not simulating or Mrs. A is not pretending are prodigious. But the propositions themselves are clear and in complete logical order.

A concrete example may make this discussion clearer.

Let: 'p' be 'Mount Hood is higher than Mount Whitney'
'q' be 'A is making sound "p"'
p and q be the propositions expressed respectively by propositional signs 'p' and 'q'
F_1 (fact 1) be 'A says p'
F_2 (fact 2) be Mr. A making a series of noises 'p'
(Let us assume that F_2 is actually the case.)
F_3 (fact 3) be the geographic fact of Mount Hood's being 11,000 feet high and Mount Whitney's being 14,000 feet

By using F_1 as a propositional sign we assert the proposition q, and thus refer to F_2; and since F_2, by hypothesis, exists, our proposition q is true. So far neither proposition p nor the fact F_3 have been involved. But if by using the propositional sign 'p' we assert proposition p, the situation changes entirely; we then deal with p and F_3; and by virtue of the character of F_3, the truth value of the proposition p happens to be falsehood.

I think I can now give an explanation of the second statement in *Tractatus*, 5.542, namely, that 'here we have no co-ordination of a fact and an object, but a co-ordination of facts by means of a co-ordination of their objects'. On the intensional interpretation of the type of propositions 'A says p', the object A was coördinated by some such relation as believing, thinking, saying, and so forth, with the proposition p. Now we coördinate the fact 'A says p' with the fact of A's saying 'p'. Remembering that 'To the configuration of the simple signs in the propositional sign corresponds the configuration of the objects in the state of affairs' (3.21), we can crudely diagram this state of affairs. And 'This shows that there is no such thing as the soul . . .' (5.5421). Indeed, no soul is discernible in this picture! But whether it could be discovered anywhere else is another matter, with which we, fortunately, are not concerned here.

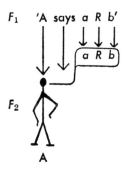

To conclude this topic we can say that general propositions and propositions of the type 'A believes p' are not exceptions to the general rule that propositions can occur in other propositions only as arguments in truth functions.

3.2 Wittgenstein's theory of truth functions has important bearing on his treatment of logic. In my discussion of Wittgenstein's logic I will make constant references to Russell. In logic Wittgenstein was a pupil of Russell, after all; and, if the pupil and the teacher disagree at times, that very disagreement may bring out the pupil's view into a clearer relief against the background of the teacher's. Wittgenstein's technical treatment of logic depends upon his view of tautology.

3.21 Among the 2^{2^n} truth functions of n atomic propositions there are two limiting cases of particular importance in a discussion on logic, namely, *tautology* and *contradiction*. Tautology is a truth function which expresses agreement with all the truth possibilities of atomic propositions involved; contradiction expresses disagreement with all of them: 'In the one case the proposition is true for all the truth-possibilities of the elementary [atomic] propositions. . . . In the second case the proposition is false for all the truth-possibilities. . . .

The tautology has no truth-conditions, for it is unconditionally true; and the contradiction is on no condition true' (4.46, 4.461). By negating a tautology we get a contradiction, and vice versa, and therefore in our discussion we may usually confine ourselves to one of them; and it is tautology that is of particular interest to us here, because Wittgenstein defines logical propositions as tautologies (6.1).

Tautology and contradiction are degenerate cases of propositions in the sense that they 'are not pictures of the reality. They present no possible state of affairs. For the one allows *every* possible state of affairs, the other *none*' (4.462). But they are important, nevertheless, because tautology 'is unconditionally true; and the contradiction is on no condition true' (4.461). Thus, while the truth of other propositions is only possible, and depends on the state of affairs in the world, 'The truth of tautology is certain, . . . of contradiction impossible' (4.464). (The 'truth' of tautology, being independent of the empirical conditions, is not an empirical truth, and it might be advisable to use some other term, say 'validity', for it rather than 'truth'; Wittgenstein, however, uses the term 'truth' for both cases, and I will generally keep his terminology.) It is this property of tautology to be certainly true independent of the truth values of its constituent atomic propositions, that is, to be 'true' a priori, that makes it so important in expressing logical propositions. In fact Wittgenstein identifies them with logical propositions: 'The propositions of logic are tautologies' (6.1); 'It is the characteristic mark of logical propositions that one can perceive in the symbol alone that they are true; and this fact contains in itself the whole philosophy of logic' (6.113). As I have already pointed out in my Chap. 2, tautologies in Wittgenstein's sense do not exhaust the possibilities of expressing logic, and in a wider sense logic is synonymous with the consistent use of any signs. For example, the proposition 'The group of signs (*a, b, c*) includes the group (*a, b*)' is not a tautology in Wittgenstein's sense; and yet it is certainly always true, that is, tautologous in a wider sense. Wittgenstein, probably, does not keep sufficiently distinct the purely formal aspects of symbolism from its application to propositions, and thus is led to the limitation of logical propositions to the truth functions of atomic propositions. In logic we need no more concern ourselves with the meaning of our symbols than we need, for the correct solution of an arithmetical sum, to think of the meaning of the groups of figures with which we work. I will not, however, pursue this controversial topic here.

Tautologies and contradictions are considered to be propositions for at least the three following reasons: first, they result automatically from the exhaustive enumeration of truth functions; second, they are constructed out of atomic propositions by the application of the same truth operation, $N(\bar{\xi})$, that is used in the construction of significant propositions; and, finally, they can be taken as arguments of truth functions, just like other propositions, counting tautologies as true and contradictions as false; for example, if p is a tautology and q a significant proposition, we can also have $p \cdot q$, $p \vee q$, and so on.

But it is important to observe that tautologies are not simply true propositions, even if they can be treated as such for certain purposes. A significant proposition asserts something about the world, and its truth depends upon the state of affairs in the world; but a tautology is a truth function constructed in such a way as to assert nothing at all about the world but to express complete ignorance concerning the truth values of the atomic propositions involved by agreeing with their every possibility. For example, the tautology 'It either rains or it does not rain now' gives us not the slightest information about the actual state of the weather, nor about anything else for that matter. It leaves us no wiser about the state of the world than we were before we heard it, and we can state it with certainty at any time without looking out a window. It is this nonsignificance of tautologies in respect to the actual state of the world that Wittgenstein has in mind when he says that tautologies or logical propositions 'are without sense' (4.461) or say nothing (5.142, 5.43). Such statements do not mean that tautologies are senseless in the sense of being absurd. Tautologies are a part of our symbolism (4.4611), and are always applicable to the world even if they do not convey any information about it (5.557). Although they ' "treat" of nothing', they 'presuppose that names have meaning, and that elementary propositions have sense. And this is their connexion with the world' (6.124).

Logical propositions could convey to us information about the world only on either of the following two conditions: (a) if logical propositions were but generalized empirical propositions, as J. S. Mill took them to be; or (b) if we could have a priori knowledge of some features of the world, as Kant would have it. But Wittgenstein rejects both these alternatives: (a) 'Theories which make a proposition of logic appear substantial are always false' (6.111); 'logical propositions can no more be empirically confirmed than they can be empirically refuted. Not only must a proposition of logic be incapable of being contradicted by any possible experience, but it must also be incapable of being confirmed by any such' (6.1222). (b) Wittgenstein also rejects Kant's view of the possibility of synthetic propositions a priori: 'There is no order of things a priori' (5.634), and 'There is no picture which is a priori true' (2.225). Thus, logic for Wittgenstein does not deal with the world either in Mill's or in Kant's sense, and therefore logical propositions do not convey to us any information about states of affairs in the world.

Logic deals only with the rules of symbolism: 'Whether a proposition belongs to logic can be calculated by logical properties of the symbol . . . ; without troubling ourselves about a sense and a meaning, we form the logical propositions out of others by mere *symbolic rules*' (6.126). Logic 'has nothing to do with the question whether our world is really of this kind or not' (6.1233); 'We cannot . . . say in logic: This and this there is in the world, that there is not' (5.61).

Logic has nothing to do either with any empirical or any miraculous characters of the world, but is merely the consistent use of our symbolism in our dealings with the world. 'The fact that the propositions of logic are tautologies *shows* the formal—logical—properties of language, of the world' (6.12); that is, it shows merely the rules of our symbolism, but it does not tell us anything about the actual state of the world.

Thus, some truth functions are tautologies or contradictions, that is, merely formal propositions; and others are significant or real propositions, asserting something or other about the facts in the world. This distinction corresponds to the traditional distinction between the analytic and the synthetic propositions, without, however, being limited to the traditional subject-predicate form, or made dependent upon the law of contradiction (which is but one of the tautologies). This distinction also corresponds to W. E. Johnson's distinction into formally certifiable and experientially certifiable propositions (*Logic,* I, Chap. IV), without, however, the psychological and metaphysical implications of Johnson's view.

3.22   Wittgenstein's view of logical propositions as tautologies, with a clearly defined meaning of tautology, offers a solution for Russell's difficulty in giving an adequate explanation of the nature of logical propositions. It is rather remarkable (but not self-contradictory on Wittgenstein's view) that such a logician as Russell could write on logic for many years before he realized that he had no sufficient criteria of what logical propositions are; but it is, nevertheless, a fact that as late as the writing of his *Introduction to Mathematical Philosophy* (published in 1918) Russell was still unable to give a sufficient definition of logical propositions. Russell thought that he found a necessary criterion of logical propositions in their formality, that is, in that they 'can be expressed wholly in terms of logical constants together with variables' (*Introduction,* p. 202). But he was aware that this criterion of logical propositions, even if necessary, was not sufficient, because there very well may be propositions which are not logical and which yet consist of nothing but logical constants and variables (*Introduction*, p. 202), for example, 'p/q'. Russell felt that a definition of logical propositions must include not merely their complete generality but also some further characteristic, and Russell called this characteristic 'tautology', but he could not give a satisfactory explanation of what it is. In Russell's own words:

> It is clear that the definition of 'logic' . . . must be sought by trying to give a new definition of the old notion of 'analytic' propositions. Although we can no longer be satisfied to define logical propositions as those that follow the law of contradiction, we can and must still admit that they are a wholly different class of propositions from those that we come to know empirically. They all have the characteristic which . . . we agreed to call 'tautology'. This, combined with the fact that they can be expressed wholly in terms of variables and logical constants (a logical constant being something which remains constant in a proposition even when *all* its constituents are changed)—will give the definition of logic. . . . For the moment I do not know how to define 'tautology'. The importance of tautology . . . was pointed out to me by my former pupil Ludwig Wittgenstein, who was working on the problem. I do not know whether he has solved it, or even whether he is alive or dead (*Introduction*, pp. 204–05).

Wittgenstein fortunately was alive, and at last succeeded in giving a clear view on the nature of tautology, thus satisfactorily resolving his teacher's difficulty. Almost all the 'asserted' propositions of *Principia Mathematica*, that is, almost all the propositions there preceded by '⊢', are tautologies.

It must be added, however, that on Wittgenstein's view, Russell's first criterion of logical propositions—that they must be propositions which can be stated by using logical terms alone—is not only not sufficient but is not even necessary: 'The mark of logical propositions is not their general validity. To be general is only to be accidentally valid for all things. An ungeneralized proposition can be tautologous just as well as a generalized one' (6.1231). True, a logical proposition or tautology is tautologous by virtue of its form alone, independent of the specific senses of the atomic propositions involved, but these senses may be, nevertheless, explicitly expressed in a logical proposition without vitiating the tautologicality of the proposition. For example, 'Mr. Smith is in this room or Mr. Smith is not in this room' is a tautology in Wittgenstein's sense, because it is of the form $p \lor \sim p$, and in spite of the fact that we actually mention several particular things in it. The factor determining tautologicality lies only in the form of a tautology, but the presence in the tautology of terms with specific meaning does not vitiate the tautologicality of the tautology. Even more, tautologies for Wittgenstein are propositions—although they are without sense, they are not nonsensical (4.461, 4.462)—and therefore it is inevitable on Wittgenstein's view that 'They presuppose that names have meaning and that elementary propositions have sense' (6.124), even if we deal with completely generalized tautologies. (As I have already said, this is, in my opinion, an unnecessary limitation of logical propositions on Wittgenstein's part.)

Of course, since a proposition is tautologous in virtue of its form alone, if we turn every constituent of it into a variable, we shall obtain another tautology, generalized but of the same form. Whether we deal with the ungeneralized or generalized tautology is, however, logically irrelevant. In works on logic it would be a waste of time to deal with particular tautologies instead of generalized ones, for example, to deal with tautologies like 'If all Greeks are men, and all men are mortal, then all Greeks are mortal', instead of $(x) \cdot \phi x \supset \psi x \cdot \psi x \supset \chi x \cdot \supset \cdot (x) \cdot \phi x \supset \chi x.$' It may also be that for some people it is psychologically more difficult to grasp the formal relations involved in a tautology dealing with particular experiences rather than those in a generalized tautology. The terseness of symbolism may be psychologically conductive to clearness for some people, even though on the other hand a mere sight of anything resembling mathematical notation has a paralyzing effect on the mentality of others. But all such considerations are practical and logically irrelevant to Wittgenstein's view on tautology. What is important here is that the tautologicality of a proposition is due to its form alone, and that therefore we can know this tautologicality through investigation of the signs expressing the proposition, without taking into account the meanings of the symbols involved, that is, without any appeal to the world; but whether the tautologies we deal with are completely generalized or are particular propositions, is logically immaterial.

3.3 Wittgenstein's view of molecular propositions as truth functions leads to a very simple theory of inference. But, before we proceed to a detailed discussion of this theory, a few general preliminary remarks should be made. First, inference for Wittgenstein is identical with formal inference or deduction. Inductive or empirical inference is for him, as for Hume, logically always accidental, is a guess, a leap into the dark; is but an elaborated and refined kind of what Russell calls physiological inference. 'All inference takes place a priori' (5.133). 'Superstition is the belief in the causal nexus' (5.1361). 'And outside logic all is accident' (6.3). 'The process of induction . . . has no logical foundation but only a psychological one' (6.363, 6.3631). 'A necessity for one thing to happen because another has happened does not exist' (6.37). Second, inference for Wittgenstein is not to be identified with the mental processes in which it may occur: 'Logic must take care of itself' (5.473); that is, logic is determined by definitions or rules and not by anything in the world, like psychological facts. Psychology is for Wittgenstein but a natural science (4.1121). As far as psychological considerations are concerned, they are simply irrelevant to a discussion of logic, and therefore of inference. Of course, if we take the term 'inference' in the more usual sense of a method by which we arrive at new knowledge, or a mental process in which a thinker actually passes from something known to something unknown, then, as Russell has repeatedly pointed out, there is 'unavoidably something psychological about inference' (for example, *Introduction to Mathematical Philosophy*, p. 149). But for Wittgenstein, inference deals only with the logical validity of such 'inference' and not with the mental processes in which it might and often does occur. Inference, for Wittgenstein, deals with what we might be tempted to call, borrowing the terms from W. E. Johnson, the constitutive aspect of the actual process in which it occurs, as contrasted with its epistemic aspect; but the whole of Johnson's logic is so permeated by psychology, epistemology, and metaphysics that I am rather wary of using his terminology. Perhaps, it would be conducive to clearness if Wittgenstein used the accepted term 'deduction' in place of his 'inference', in order to keep it distinct from inductive inference on one hand and psychological considerations on the other.

3.31   Wittgenstein states the essentials of his view on inference as follows:

Those truth-possibilities of its truth-arguments, which verify the proposition, I shall call its *truth-grounds*. If the truth-grounds which are common to a number of propositions are all also truth-grounds of some one proposition, we say that the truth of this proposition follows from the truth of those propositions. In particular the truth of a proposition p follows from that of a proposition q, if all the truth-grounds of the second are truth-grounds of the first. The truth-grounds of q are contained in those of p; p follows from q. If p follows from q, the sense of 'p' is contained in that of 'q' (5.101–5.122).

In other words, the truth grounds of a proposition are those truth possibilities of its constituent propositions with which the proposition agrees, and not those with which it disagrees. And the proposition p follows from, or is inferable from, the proposition q, if all truth grounds of q are contained in the truth grounds of p; which means that p is inferable from q, if p agrees with all those truth possibilities of its constituent propositions with which q also agrees, while the converse is left undetermined; that is, p may also agree with some additional truth possibilities. If p follows from q and vice versa (if p agrees with all the truth possibilities with which q agrees, and vice versa), then p and q 'are one and the same proposition' (5.141).

In *T-F* notation (Table 6) 'p follows from q' is shown by the fact that to every T of q there corresponds a T in p, regardless of what other T's p may also happen to have. In somewhat more familiar language the proposition 'p follows from q' may be expressed as '$q \, . \sim p$ is self-contradictory', because p cannot be false when q is true if we agree that to every T of q there also corresponds a T of p; in another form this can be expressed as '$\sim (q \, . \sim p)$ is tautologous', or as '$q \supset p$ is tautologous'. Similarly, 'p follows from q' may be also expressed as '$q \, . \, p$ is equivalent to q', or more compactly as $q \, . \, p \, \cdot \equiv \cdot \, q$ because the truth grounds of q are the same as those which are common to q and to p. This form suggests in a tangible way how the truth grounds of q are 'contained' in those of p; q cannot be true unless p is also true. There are, of course, many other expressions for 'p follows q', but the above seem to be among the most convenient.

For the sake of clearness it may be pointed out here that 'from an elementary [atomic] proposition no other can be inferred' (5.134); 'other' here must mean 'other atomic', because it is possible to make an inference from an atomic proposition to a molecular one, for example, '$p \vee q$ follows from p', even if p is atomic. However, the inferred proposition must be molecular except for the special case of inferring a proposition from itself. To avoid confusion we might for the sake of convenience on certain occasions write capital letters for the molecular propositions when these are used in inference, and reserve small letters for their arguments; to simplify the notation we might even use only one capital letter with subscripts for the molecular propositions involved, and one small letter with subscripts for their arguments. Then we could write 'P_1 follows from P_2', if to every T of P_2 there corresponds a T of P_1, where, for example, P_1 is $p \lor q$ or $p_1 \lor p_2$, and P_2 is $p \cdot q$ or $p_1 \cdot p_2$, and so forth. I will resort to this notation on occasions when it may help to make the exposition clearer, but I do not intend to follow it always, because in some cases it would make matters more confusing than otherwise, for example, when it may conflict with the notation in quotations from the *Tractatus*.

That the inference 'P_1 follows from P_2' depends on the connection between the truth grounds of P_1 and P_2 may be expressed also by saying that P_1 and P_2 are internally or structurally connected: 'That the truth of one proposition follows from the truth of other propositions, we perceive from the structure of the propositions. If the truth of one proposition follows from the truth of others, this expresses itself in relations in which the forms of these propositions stand to one another' (5.13, 5.131). 'The structures of propositions stand to one another in internal relations' (5.2). The main point in inference we have to stress here is that it proceeds formally, and depends only on the connection between the forms of the truth functions involved, and not on the specific senses of their arguments: 'All inference takes place a priori' (5.133). Thus, if P_2 be $p_1 \cdot p_2$ and P_1 be $p_1 \lor p_2$, then P_1 follows from P_2 because of their internal connection—because of the ways P_1 and P_2 are built up by logical operations from p_1 and p_2, or, to put it in another way, because the truth grounds of $P_1(TTT-)$ contain the truth grounds of $P_2(T---)$, regardless of what senses p_1 and p_2 have.

But here we must observe that, while the inference is due only to the formal relations between truth functions and regardless of the senses of their arguments, these senses are nevertheless present in the truth functions involved in the inference. When we infer P_1 from P_2, we infer the sense of P_1

from the sense of P_2 as well: 'if p follows from q, the sense of "p" is contained in that of "q"' (5.122). If P_3 and P_4 happen to be the same truth functions of p_3 and p_4 as P_1 and P_2 are of p_1 and p_2, then P_3 follows from P_4 in the same way as P_1 follows from P_2, but the senses involved in two inferences are different. The sense of $p_1 \vee p_2$ is contained in the the sense of $p_1 . p_2$, and the sense of $p_3 \vee p_4$ is contained in the same way in the sense of $p_3 . p_4$; but the sense of $p_1 \vee p_2$ is not contained in the sense of $p_3 . p_4$, and the sense of $p_3 . p_4$ is not contained in the sense of $p_1 . p_2$. The connection between the senses of P_1 and of P_2 can perhaps be made clearer by the following consideration: 'P_2 follows from P_1' is formally equivalent to $P_1 \equiv : P_1 . P_2$, and the latter can be read as 'Stating the sense of P_1 is equivalent to stating the sense of $P_1 . P_2$'. In regard to sense, the term 'contain' means the relation of the more specific sense to the less specific one: 'If a proposition follows from another, then the latter says more than the former, the former less than the latter' (5.14). For example, the sense of $p \vee q$ is contained in the sense of $p . q$, because $p . q$ says more than, is more specific than, $p \vee q$; $p . q$ says that p and q are both true, while $p \vee q$ says merely that 'at least one, p or q, is true, and it may be that both of them are'; the first one not only gives us all the information that the second one gives, but it also gives more. We may notice in passing that Wittgenstein's term 'contain' applies to the truth grounds of two propositions in just the reverse way from its application to the senses of the same propositions; if 'P_2 follows from P_1', then the truth grounds of P_1 are contained in the truth grounds of P_2 (to every T of P_1 there is a corresponding T in P_2, but P_2 may also have other T's), and the sense of P_2 is contained in the sense of P_1.

I will give a few examples of inference from Table 6. Truth function No. 5 (*TTTF*) follows from No. 8 (*FTTF*) but not conversely. Table 7 shows this graphically. Here to every T of No. 8 there corresponds a T of No. 5. Similarly, No. 5

TABLE 7

		No. 5	No. 8
p	q	$p \lor q$	$p . \sim q : \lor : \sim p . q$
T	T	T	F
F	T	$T \longleftarrow$	$< T$
T	F	$T \longleftarrow$	$< T$
F	F	F	F

follows from Nos. 10, 11, 13, 14, and 15. On the other hand, No. 5 does not follow from, for example, No. 6. Table 8

TABLE 8

		No. 5	No. 6
p	q	$p \lor q$	$\sim q$
T	T	T	F
F	T	T	F
T	F	$T \longleftarrow$	T
F	F	$F \longleftarrow\cdots$	$\cdots T$

shows this graphically. Here to one of the T's of No. 6 corresponds T of No. 5, but to the other T of No. 6 corresponds F of No. 5; No. 5 may be false while No. 6 is true and, therefore, No. 5 does not follow from No. 6.

Propositions which have no T in common 'are opposed to one another' (5.1241); they may, however, have F's in common. Propositions which have neither T's nor F's in common contradict or deny each other (5.1241). For example, in Table 9 No. 5 contradicts No. 12; No. 7 opposes Nos. 10, 13, and 15. Opposition, as in traditional logic, is rather a loose

TABLE 9

		No. 5	No. 12	No. 7	No. 10	No. 13	No. 15
p	q	$p \lor q$	$\sim p . \sim q$	$\sim p$	p	$p . \sim q$	$p . q$
T	T	$T \cdots$	$\cdots\rightarrow F$	F	T	F	T
F	T	$T \cdots$	$\cdots\rightarrow F$	$T \cdots$	$\cdots F \cdots$	$\cdots F$	$\cdots\rightarrow F$
T	F	$T \cdots$	$\cdots\rightarrow F$	F	T	T	F
F	F	$F \longleftarrow\cdots$	$\cdots T$	$T \cdots$	$\cdots F \cdots$	$\cdots F$	$\cdots\rightarrow F$

relation; thus, while No. 7 opposes Nos. 10, 13, and 15, Nos. 10 and 13 do not oppose each other, and neither do Nos. 10 and 15; and Nos. 7 and 10 contradict each other, but no other pairs do. Strangely, Wittgenstein does not use the traditional term 'contrary', which is useful and would fit nicely into his scheme. 'Propositions which have no truth-arguments in common' are independent (5.152); that is, propositions which have no atomic components in common are independent, and all atomic propositions are mutually independent.

Tautology and contradiction are limiting cases, and they contradict or deny one another. In connection with tautologies and contradictions all inference is trivial. Contradiction has no truth grounds, and therefore its truth grounds are vacuously contained in any proposition; any proposition follows from it vacuously, to borrow a convenient term from mathematics. To put this in a less puzzling way, 'p follows from q' is equivalent to '$\sim p \cdot q$ is a contradiction', but if q is itself a contradiction then $\sim p \cdot q$ must also be a contradiction no matter what p is. Thus we can say that 'p follows from q' no matter what p is, as long as q is a contradiction. A tautology can be inferred from any proposition, and from a tautology only a tautology follows (5.142, 6.126). Thus, let p be a significant proposition and q a tautology; we can form the logical product $p \cdot q$ which is equivalent to p, since q is a tautology: 'The logical product of a tautology and a proposition says the same as the proposition' (4.465); and q of course follows from $p \cdot q$, and thus a tautology q is inferred from a significant proposition p. Similarly, if p is a tautology, we can form the logical product of p and any other tautology, and then formally and trivially deduce from this product that other tautology.

3.32 Wittgenstein does not offer any special name for the converse of the relation of 'follows', that is, for the relation that q has to p if 'p follows from q'. I will adopt for this relation the term 'tautologically implies'. I do not wish to use

G. E. Moore's term 'entails', because I do not want to raise the question whether Moore and Wittgenstein mean the same thing by 'follow'; I think they do not. C. I. Lewis' 'strict implication' is a different notion, based upon impossibility as a value of propositions distinct from truth and falsity; but in logic, according to Wittgenstein, we need no other values of propositions except truth and falsehood. Russell's 'formal implication' is but a class or aggregate of material implications, and differs from material implication only by introduction of generality. I will discuss the relation between tautological and material implications in some detail. 'Tautological implication' is an appropriate name for the relation under consideration, because this relation is nothing but the major 'material' implication in a tautology. Then, whenever 'p follows from q', we can write '$q \supset p$ tautologically', where '$\supset$' is Russell's material implication. And I propose to write this more compactly as $q \ \overline{T} \ p$, where '$\overline{T}$' is a combination of 'T' and '$\supset$' and stands for 'implies tautologically'.

3.321   There is an interesting connection as well as an unfortunate confusion between tautological implication and what Russell calls 'material implication' or simply 'implication', and symbolizes by '$\supset$' ('horseshoe'). An enormous amount of bitter and mostly fruitless controversy about '$\supset$' would not have taken place if Russell used the term 'horseshoe' instead of the misleading 'material implication'. $p \supset q$ is defined by Russell as 'Either p is false or q is true' (*Principia*, p. 94); that is, $p \supset q$ is that truth function of p and of q which has truth value T if p is true and q is true, or p is false and q is true, or p is false and q is false, and which has truth value F if p is true but q is false. In fact, it is nothing but the truth function No. 4 of our Table 6 (p. 121) and may happen to hold even when both p and q are atomic, as well as when either or both of them are molecular. '$p \supset q$ tautologically' means 'q follows from p', and it holds only when there is some formal relation between p and q such that 'the truth grounds of p are contained in those of q'; p in '$p \supset q$ tautologically' must be molecular, except in the limiting case where we infer p from itself.

The connection between tautological implication and material implication is this: material implication ($\supset$) becomes tautological (Ⅎ) when it occurs as the major implication in a tautology. Thus, we can express 'P implies Q tautologically' as '$P \supset Q$ is a tautology' or $P \ \text{Ⅎ} \ Q$. For example, $p \supset q$. p : $\supset q$ is a tautology, because the second '$\supset$' is tautological; that is, $p \supset q$. p: $\text{Ⅎ} \ q$. Furthermore, whenever we have 'P implies Q tautologically', that is, '$P \supset Q$ is a tautology', we also have simply $P \supset Q$, that is, 'P materially implies Q'. In other words, $P \ \text{Ⅎ} \ Q$ implies tautologically that $P \supset Q$. But while we can always substitute '$\supset$' for 'tautological implication', the converse does not hold, and therefore the two relations are not equivalent. 'Ⅎ' is a stronger relation than '$\supset$'. This is due to the fact that tautological implication is a formal or internal relation between the propositions involved, while material implication is external or accidental to them. In $p \ \text{Ⅎ} \ q$, p and q must be internally or formally connected, so that from p alone we could infer q; and it is obvious that q here must be molecular, except in the limiting case of q's being identical with p. But in $p \supset q$, p and q may be logically entirely independent; for example, both may be atomic. In $p \ \text{Ⅎ} \ q$ the implicate follows from the implicans; in $p \supset q$ the implicate does not necessarily follow from the implicans.

Even Russell is not free from confusing $p \supset q$ with '$p \supset q$ tautologically', and thus from committing what G. E. Moore characterized as the 'enormous howler' of using 'p materially implies q' in the sense of 'q can be deduced from p'. Thus, for example, Russell says: 'in order that one proposition may be inferred from another, it is necessary that the two should have that relation which makes the one a consequence of the other. When a proposition q is a consequence of a proposition p, we say that p implies q' (*Principia*, p. 90). Here Russell uses the term 'inference' in the same sense as Wittgenstein, that is, as deduction. But Russell's 'material implication' or 'horseshoe' is defined as 'Either p is false or q is true' (*Principia*, p. 94). Thus, Russell says in substance that 'q is deducible from p' and '$p \supset q$' are equivalent, which is a 'howler'. Moreover, '$\supset$' is but one of many possible truth relations between propositions, and is in no way more fundamental than any other; in fact, in *Principia* it is not even taken as a primitive idea, but is defined in terms of negation and disjunction, and therefore it may be entirely eliminated from *Principia* without affecting any of the deductions in that work. But if it were necessary for these deductions, and yet we can rewrite the whole of *Principia* without it, *Principia* contains no deduction! Russell certainly does not mean that; and he does not mean either that negation and disjunction, to which '$\supset$' can be reduced, are indispensable for deduction. He simply confuses the two meanings of 'implies': '$\supset$' and '$\supset$ tautologically'. Almost all the propositions of *Principia* are tautologies with variable arguments, and Russell may, of course, write '$\supset$' wherever the implication is tautologous, because material implication, as I have pointed out, follows from tautological implication. In practice Russell does not confuse the two, but the two concepts should be distinguished. In fact, they are distinguished in *Principia* by the sign '$\vdash$' prefixed to tautologies. Russell himself reads '$\vdash$' as 'it is true that' or 'it is asserted that', but, as H. M. Sheffer points out, it would be better to read it as 'it is necessary that', and in our terminology we may read it as 'it is tautologous that'.

3.322   The form '$p \supset q$ tautologically' for 'q follows from p' is very convenient for a practical checking of the validity of inference:

If for example two propositions 'p' and 'q' give a tautology in the connexion '$p \supset q$', then it is clear that q follows from p. E.g. that q follows from '$p \supset q . p$' we see from these two propositions themselves, but we can also show it by combining them to '$p \supset q . p : \supset : q$' and then showing that this is a tautology (6.1221).

In the last example, the first '⊃' is the material implication, and the second is the tautological implication. We could write the second as $p \supset q . p : Ƃ : q$. Table 10 shows this graphically.

Table 10

p	q	$p \supset q$	P_1 $\overbrace{p \supset q . p}$	P_1 $\overbrace{p \supset q . p : Ƃ q}$
T	T	T	T	$T \supset T = T$
F	T	T	F	$F \supset T = T$
T	$F.$	F	F	$F \supset F = T$
F	F	T	F	$F \supset F = T$

Let us illustrate this method of testing the validity of inference between propositions with a rather complicated case. Let us take *3.47 of *Principia*, namely, $p \supset r . q \supset s . \supset : p . q . \supset . r . s$. To facilitate the procedure we can group the constituents of this expression into relatively simple complexes, and then proceed to the more complex constituents, and so on, until the whole expression is reached determining at each step the truth conditions of each complex by reference to the truth conditions of their constituents. The major implication here is the third one, and we are to see whether it is tautological. This process is arranged graphically in Table 11. We see from the last column of this table that '$P_3 \supset P_6$ tautologically', and that therefore $p . q . \supset . r . s$ does follow from $p \supset r . q \supset s$ and so we may write $p \supset r . q \supset s . Ƃ : p . q . \supset . r . s$.

We must not, however, think that by putting our propositions into the form of a tautology we arrive at something new concerning these propositions. We must not confuse the merely practical convenience or the psychological novelty of the result of our manipulation of symbols with the logical validity of inference. That P_2 follows from P_1 does not depend on P_1 and P_2 being put into the explicit tautology $P_1 Ƃ P_2$; it is only our

TABLE 11

An illustration of evaluation of a proposition with four atomic elements

$$p \supset r . q \supset s . \supset : p . q . \supset . r . s$$

	p	q	r	s	P_1 $p \supset r$	P_2 $q \supset s$	$P_3 = . P_1 . P_2$ $p \supset r . q \supset s$	P_4 $p . q$	P_5 $r . s$	$P_6 = . P_4 \supset P_5$ $p . q . \supset . r . s$	$P_3 \supset P_6$
1	T	T	T	T	T	T	T	T	T	T	T
2	F	T	T	T	T	T	T	F	T	T	T
3	T	F	T	T	T	T	T	F	T	T	T
4	F	F	T	T	T	T	T	F	T	T	T
5	T	T	F	T	F	T	F	T	F	F	T
6	F	T	F	T	T	T	T	F	F	T	T
7	T	F	F	T	F	T	F	F	F	T	T
8	F	F	F	T	T	T	T	F	F	T	T
9	T	T	T	F	T	F	F	T	F	F	T
10	F	T	T	F	T	F	F	F	F	T	T
11	T	F	T	F	T	T	T	F	F	T	T
12	F	F	T	F	T	T	T	F	F	T	T
13	T	T	F	F	F	F	F	T	F	F	T
14	F	T	F	F	T	F	F	F	F	T	T
15	T	F	F	F	F	T	F	F	F	T	T
16	F	F	F	F	T	T	T	F	F	T	T

psychological capacity for recognition of this relation that may happen to be dependent upon such devices. All that is logically necessary for inference from P_1 to P_2 is that the truth grounds of P_1 be contained in those of P_2. The rest is logically irrelevant: 'Proof in logic is only a mechanical expedient to facilitate the recognition of tautology, where it is complicated' (6.1262). A 'proof' in logic merely displays the syntax of our symbolism. 'Proof,' said G. H. Hardy, 'is but a rhetorical flourish'.

There is no need for rules of inference in logic: 'The method of inference is to be understood from the two propositions alone. Only they themselves can justify the inferences. Laws of inference, which—as in Frege and Russell—are to justify the conclusions, are senseless and would be superfluous' (*Tractatus,* 5.132). Inference depends merely on whether the truth grounds of one of the propositions are contained among the truth grounds of the other, and this formal relation between the two propositions can be recognized directly from them, without combining them into a tautology: 'We can get on without logical propositions, for we can recognize in an adequate notation the formal properties of the propositions by mere inspection' (6.122).

Moreover, though 'q follows from p' does not mean that q is true, unless in addition we also know that p is true, the inference from p to q is independent of such additional empirical information about the truth values of the propositions involved. The inference in Wittgenstein's sense depends only on the formal relation between the truth grounds of the propositions, and not on their truth values. We can say 'we infer correctly, because there is a such-and-such formal relation between these two symbols'; and this formal relation must be known to us as soon as we understand these propositions, without any further knowledge of their truth values. But we cannot say, 'we infer correctly because this and this is true'. Inference is due to the grammatical determinations of our language and not to the actual state of affairs in the world:

'All inference takes place a priori' (5.133). Inference for Wittgenstein is deduction.

We can see now that the term 'inference' is used in the *Tractatus* in a sense different from Russell's. Russell says: 'The process of inference is as follows: a proposition "p" is asserted, and a proposition "p implies q" is asserted, and then as a sequel the proposition "q" is asserted' (*Principia,* pp. 8–9). That is, in inference, according to Russell, we assert p and $p \supset q$ and then q. It appears as if in order to make an inference one needed to know the truth values of the premises. But, as I have just pointed out, on Wittgenstein's view we do not need to know the truth values of the premise in inference. All we have to know is the truth grounds of the premise and the conclusion, and the relation between the two. It may be even the case that the premise is false: 'One can *draw conclusions* from a false proposition' (*Tractatus,* 4.023). All inference proceeds a priori, that is, without appeal to the actual truth or falsity of the propositions, and depends only upon the formal relations between propositions. Furthermore, if 'q follows from p', then $p \supset q$ in Russell's schema of inference does not play the role which Russell seems to assign to it, namely, the role of a proposition additional and different from p and yet necessary for inference from p to q; $p \supset q$ is merely a grammatical transformation of p in order to bring it into Russell's schema, $p \cdot p \supset q : \supset q$. It is but a grammatical insertion piece, not essential to the formal relation between p and q by virtue of which we can infer q from p. It is the inference from p to q that is under consideration, and not an inference from p together with some other proposition, say r (in our case $p \supset q$), to q. The addition of some proposition other than p to p, say r, would change our premise p; we would then be inferring from $p \cdot r$ to q, and not from p to q. Inference proceeds from p alone to q alone, and $p \supset q$ is but a grammatical analysis of p, and not a new premise. In the process of inference it is not essential to bring our propositions into the schema $p \cdot p \supset q : \supset q$. What is essential is that there be a connection between the truth grounds of p and q such that the truth grounds of p are contained among those of q. The rest is but a rhetorical flourish.

This view of the nature of inference will have bearing on Wittgenstein's criticism of *Principia*, my next topic, but I wish to make a brief remark here on the disagreement between Russell and Wittgenstein. In answering Wittgenstein's criticism Russell could say that the controversy is at least partly verbal. What Wittgenstein calls 'inference' Russell calls 'implication'. And Russell would agree that his 'inference' is not a purely logical notion. In fact Russell definitely holds that 'There is always unavoidably *something* psychological about inference, and what is not psychological about it is the relation which allows us to infer correctly' (*Introduction to Mathematical Philosophy*, p. 149). And it is this 'relation which allows us to infer correctly' that Wittgenstein chooses to call 'inference'. I do not wish to become involved in this verbal controversy (although I am inclined to take Russell's side here), but in the following section will use the term 'inference' with the meaning given to it in the *Tractatus*.

3.4 In the light of Wittgenstein's view of logic, logical propositions, and inference, as expounded in this essay, we can now criticize a possible misinterpretation of *Principia Mathematica*.

3.41 *Principia* begins with undefined or "primitive" ideas (elements and relations) and propositions. By means of these ideas and propositions it then claims to define all other ideas of logic and eventually of mathematics; and by means of the primitive propositions used as substantive premises on the one hand, and as the formal rules of deduction on the other, it proposes to deduce all the logical propositions needed for the construction of all mathematics. The internal validity of *Principia* as a deductive system is a matter for detailed investigation. Russell himself is not quite satisfied with it on this score, for example, on account of the omission of an enunciation of the nonformal principle of inference used there, and on account of the presence of the notorious axiom of reducibility. I will be concerned here only with the principles underlying the *Principia* as a logical system.

Principia has been criticized as a mathematical or deductive postulational system by several people, notably by B. A. Bernstein and H. M. Sheffer. Bernstein criticized *Principia* on the ground that its primitive propositions or postulates do not bring out the properties of its undefined ideas and that *Principia* instead reads them into the system 'unofficially', from outside the system, while claiming that it makes all its assumptions explicit (see, for example, *Principia*, p. 90). In a deductive postulational system the postulates are implicit definitions of the undefined ideas of the system; and the system itself has to be considered in the context of the general unsymbolized logic underlying it and the language in which it is written. The principles of logic cannot be defined explicitly, and are taken for granted from 'outside' the system. I think Bernstein is right in his criticism of *Principia* as a deductive postulational system.[1]

But Russell would probably answer this criticism by saying that it is beside the point. He might say, perhaps, that *Principia* is not a postulational deductive system, but is a self-contained deductive system of logic itself, and that mathematics can be deduced from it without using any ideas or propositions outside the *Principia*. Russell might say that the 'primitive' propositions of the *Principia* are not arbitrary postulates, but are logical propositions or tautologies, and therefore they implicitly contain the general logical principles. Logic is thus formally 'inside' this system itself, and *Principia* does not need any other general logic to underlie it. Psychologically, Russell may add, we may have difficulty in reading *Principia*, and we need, as an accident of existence, to know English to

---

[1] In the *Bulletin of the American Mathematical Society*, Vol. XXXVII, No. 6, Bernstein proposes a way of transforming *Principia* into a mathematical postulational system. I am not, however, concerned with that here.

get on to it. 'The primitive ideas are *explained* by means of descriptions intended to point out to the reader what is meant; but the explanations do not constitute definitions, because they really involve the ideas they explain' (*Principia*, p. 91). And logical propositions of *Principia* need no outside logical help for being just what they are, namely, tautologies. From the primitive logical propositions as premises, and by means of them as formal rules of deduction, we can deduce step by step all the other logical propositions of *Principia*, and ultimately all the mathematical propositions, without further help of any 'outside' logic. Perhaps *Principia* as it stands is not as self-contained as it was intended to be, and then it has to be supplemented. Russell himself suggests this, for example, concerning his nonformal principle of deduction (what Johnson calls applicative principle). But this is a defect of detail, and does not affect the validity of the view underlying *Principia*. Thus, Russell might say, *Principia* is not intended to be merely a postulational deductive system, like Euclidean geometry, because its 'primitive' propositions are not postulates but are logical propositions. *Principia* then appears to be a deductive system of logical propositions; it is built up out of propositions accepted intuitively as tautologous, by means of explicitly stated (with some unfortunate shortcomings) intuitively certain rules and principles of inference.

3.42 The main criticism here from Wittgenstein's point of view is that logic is not a system. *Principia* says: Out of these primitive propositions taken as axioms follow these and these tautologies as theorems. But *Principia* is limited to the enumerated set of tautologies systematically arranged, and it is but one of innumerable possible deductive systems differing from the others only by having for its primitive propositions certain logical propositions. But what is essential to logic is that logic is authoritative for all tautologies and all deductions, not merely those in a particular system. Logic is common to all systems of symbolism and cannot be identified with any one symbolic expression of it. To consider logic by analogy with postulational deductive systems is misleading, and would lead to the absurd notion of the plurality of logics, just as there is a plurality of geometries. Of course, logical propositions can be arranged into a system, in fact into any number of systems, because logical propositions or tautologies follow from all propositions (*Tractatus,* 5.142), including any arbitrarily chosen set of 'primitive' tautologies. But the tautologicality of logical propositions does not depend upon their place in any such system; it depends only upon their own form. 'Every tautology itself shows that it is a tautology' (6.127). In a word, logic is not a deductive system. Considering the importance of this subject, it may be worthwhile to elaborate on it a little.

There is logically no essential difference between the 'primitive' and deduced propositions of logic in any system: 'All propositions of logic are of equal rank; there are not some which are essentially primitive and others deduced from these' (6.127). Russell himself mentions that 'It is to some extent optional what . . . we take as undefined' (*Principia,* p. 91). Wittgenstein goes further and says that it is *entirely* optional which of the tautologies we take as primitives. But they must be tautologies and not merely postulates. The distinction between axioms and theorems of a system does not hold in logic; all logical propositions are on the same logical level. The choice of the 'primitives' and the order of deduction of logical 'theorems' are perfectly arbitrary; the hierarchical order of the logical propositions of *Principia* is logically unessential and is completely external to these propositions. Each tautology stands as tautology in its own right and not as a consequence of some other tautology chosen as 'primitive'. Of course, these remarks are not intended to invalidate Russell's deductions in *Principia.* They merely point out that those deductions are logically superfluous for the tautological character of the tautologies deduced from the 'primitive' tautologies. Propositions of *Principia* are tautologies because of their form, and their position in the artificial deductive arrangement of *Principia* is logically accidental to them: 'We prove a logical proposition by creating it out of other logical propositions by applying in succession certain operations, which again generate tautologies out of the first. . . . This way of showing that its propositions are tautologies is quite unessential to logic' (*Tractatus*, 6.126). 'Proof in logic is only a mechanical expedient to facilitate the recognition of tautology, where it is complicated' (6.1262).

The same thing can be seen from consideration of the role of deduction of one logical proposition from another. Deduction here is merely a notational transformation of one tautology into another. We merely repeat the same thing in a different way. And this is not the same as deducing a theorem from an axiom in a postulational deductive system. In such a system a theorem and an axiom are not equivalent: we cannot deduce an axiom from a theorem without changing the system. A theorem follows from an axiom as one significant proposition follows from another, and is not a mere notational transformation of the axiom. Deduction between tautologies is a limiting or degenerate case of deduction, and it does not lead to any system or hierarchical order between tautologies. The serial order of tautologies in *Principia* is not due to any intrinsic deductive logical order between tautologies. Thus, again we conclude that *Principia Mathematica* as an exemplification of logic is not a postulational deductive system.

That the 'primitive' propositions of *Principia* do not play the role of axioms in a postulational deductive system may be seen also in another way. Let us ask what would happen if we denied some of the 'primitives'. If the axioms of a deductive system are denied, the system is invalidated. But would the logic of *Principia* be invalidated or changed into some other non-Russellian logic if we denied some of the primitive propositions of *Principia*? Not at all. We either would not obtain any logical propositions in *Principia* at all, or we would obtain the logical propositions of the same old logic, provided that the rules of our notation were appropriately changed. For example, if we wrote '$\vdash : \sim (q \supset . p \lor q)$' instead of '$\vdash : q \supset . p \lor q$' (*Principia*, *1.3), we would get either a contradiction, a significant proposition, or a tautology, depending on how we were going to interpret the signs '$\sim$', '$\lor$', and '$\supset$'. We do not get any new logic here.

3.43   To conclude this discussion of *Principia,* we can say that, considered as an exemplification or an expression of logic it is not a postulational deductive system. *Principia* is an arbitrary collection of logical propositions or tautologies artificially arranged in a practically convenient order. In imposing this order the authors were guided by the psychological obviousness of some logical propositions; by the purpose of showing how we can define all the existing mathematical ideas by means of certain 'primitive' ideas, and deduce all the known mathematical theorems from and by means of certain 'primitive' logical propositions; and by such historical accidents as works on logic and mathematics, especially by Peano and Frege, and the whole body of the existing mathematics. Otherwise, why should *Principia* contain just those particular logical propositions which it does contain, instead of any other of the innumerable possible logical propositions? And why does it have the particular order it happens to have, rather than any other possible order?

All this is not to say that the deductions of *Principia* are invalid. The validity of *Principia* is a matter for detailed investigation. All that this discussion tries to bring out is that logic is not intrinsically a deductive system of true propositions, and that the systematic deductive order of *Principia* is a practical convenience for the purpose of deducing already existing mathematics from logical propositions, but is not essential to logic. To what extent *Principia* succeeded in deducing mathematical propositions from logical propositions is another and very interesting matter, with which I am, however, not concerned here.

Wittgenstein's Philosophy

I have discussed various aspects of Wittgenstein's view on language or symbolism. For several reasons I will omit from my discussion a number of interesting and important subjects treated in the *Tractatus,* such as mathematics, natural science, and ethics. And I will close with a discussion of Wittgenstein's view on philosophy.

All philosophy is 'Critique of language' (4.0031). Philosophy is not one of the natural sciences. (The word 'philosophy' must mean something which stands above or below, but not beside the natural sciences.) The object of philosophy is the logical clarification of thoughts. Philosophy is not a theory but an activity. A philosophical work consists essentially of elucidations. The result of philosophy is not a number of 'philosophical propositions', but to make propositions clear. Philosophy should make clear and delimit sharply the thoughts which otherwise are, as it were, opaque and blurred (4.111, 4.112).

4.1   Philosophy is not a body of knowledge. Neither is it a theory about the world based upon empirical investigation; nor is it a special knowledge of the ultimate nature of reality, obtained a priori or by some extra-empirical revelation. It is but an activity of clarifying our language. In other words, *philosophy is a pursuit of meaning and sense,* and not of truth. The latter pursuit is the business of science and everyday life. Thus, on Wittgenstein's view philosophy has two fundamental characteristics: First of all, it is an activity, and not a set of propositions. Second, this activity is directed not to the search for truth, but to making our language clear.

The task of a philosopher is to see that all discourse complies with the following two conditions: (a) that it contain only the terms which have unique and unambiguous *meaning* for the purpose in hand and under the given circumstances, this meaning being assigned either by explicit definitions or by pointing; and (b) that its propositions be constructed according to the rules of our language, so as to make determinate *sense.* It is the duty of a philosopher to see that these conditions are complied with in all actual uses of language, in everyday life, and in science, science being but an extension of everyday life to more difficult and general cases. It was a philosophical work on the part of Aristotle to point out the ambiguity of the word 'is', and then to try to eliminate this ambiguity. The whole task of philosophy is confined to the particular task of eliminating confusion in language, whenever and wherever such confusion arises. This task is endless, because we constantly create new terms and make new propositions, and there is no limit to our future experience and therefore to our propositions about it. Moreover, we need not take any of the results of our clarification as final; it is possible that on further investigation we can clarify and sharpen our language still further. But the unchanging purpose of all philosophizing is to make our language clear and unambiguous; to reject as meaningless all the statements for which we can find no determinate meaning, and to make as clear and precise as we can those statements which are vague and ambiguous. In philosophy we deal with the rules of our language and not with what this language is about: in philosophy we can only make clear to ourselves which rules we want to follow.

In this view of philosophy Wittgenstein is essentially in

agreement with Socrates, as far as Socrates' practice but not his theory is concerned. Socrates' method was not to give any information, but to make clear what was meant by certain questions concerning human nature and conduct. It is not the subject matter dealt with by Socrates, namely, ethical problems, that is important here, but the method he used to investigate this subject matter, because, according to Wittgenstein, this method is the right method of philosophy when dealing with any subject matter whatsoever. The method consists in the attempts to make clear the sense of the propositions under consideration. Socrates, of course, went farther, and claimed that by the persistent application of this method, and only by this method, we can arrive at least at some ethical truths. The rationalistic metaphysics of Socrates is due to his confusion of the activity of clarification of language with the investigation of the world. Wittgenstein accepts Socratic practice as sound philosophy, but he rejects his metaphysical theory. Wittgenstein expresses this modernized version of the restricted Socratic view as follows:

The right method of philosophy would be this. To say nothing except what can be said, *i.e.* the propositions of natural science, *i.e.* something that has nothing to do with philosophy: and then always, when someone else wished to say something metaphysical, to demonstrate to him that he had given no meaning to certain signs in his propositions. This method would be unsatisfying to the other—he would not have the feeling that we were teaching him philosophy—but it would be the only strictly correct method (6.53).

The trouble with Socrates was that he was not sufficiently Socratic!

Wittgenstein's view of philosophy is a natural development of Russell's view, but Wittgenstein goes farther than Russell in condemnation of the traditional philosophy, and it may be instructive to compare Wittgenstein's view on this point with that of his teacher. Russell's intention, as expressed in the lectures collected in the volume *Our Knowledge of the External*

World, was to base philosophy upon science. Now this can be done (as Russell further points out in *Mysticism and Logic,* p. 98), in either of two ways. First, philosophy may be based on the most general *results* of science, and it will then consist of the generalization and unification of these results. Or, second, philosophy may adopt the *methods* of science and 'seek to apply these methods, with necessary adaptations, to its own peculiar province'. Russell chooses the second view: 'It is not results, but *methods,* that can be transferred with profit from the sphere of the special sciences to the sphere of philosophy' (*Mysticism and Logic,* p. 98). Of course, the mere adoption of the methods of science will affect the range and the kind of problems capable of investigation. All metaphysics will be ruled out; thus Russell points out that the notion of the universe is to be ruled out from the province of philosophy. And, concerning the empirical investigation of the world, philosophy has nothing to add to science: 'Philosophy is not a short cut to the same kind of results as those of the other sciences: if it is to be a genuine study, it must have a province of its own, and aim at results which the other sciences can neither prove nor disprove' (*Knowledge of External World,* p. 17). But— and here is a very important difference between Russell and Wittgenstein—for Russell there still remains a special province of philosophy. For Russell science and philosophy, while using essentially the same method, apply it to different spheres of human knowledge. Philosophy, 'when it is purified from all practical taint, is to help us to understand the general aspects of the world' (*Knowledge of External World,* p. 17). 'Philosophy . . . becomes indistinguishable from logic' (*Mysticism and Logic,* p. 111). The special province of philosophy is then logic, and philosophy is but a science of logic. But, as we saw in my previous chapter, for Wittgenstein there is no science of logic, and therefore there is no philosophy as defined by Russell.

Wittgenstein agrees with Russell that fundamentally there is no other way of obtaining truth than the way of science, that is, by observing facts and reflecting upon the data so obtained, and that philosophy has no special and superior method of attaining truth. But Wittgenstein does not agree with Russell's view that philosophy is a science with a special nonempirical domain. Systematic search for truth in *any* domain is science for Wittgenstein, and we cannot consider philosophy as a separate science fundamentally distinct from all other sciences merely on the ground of the peculiarity of its subject matter. Thus, if philosophy is fundamentally distinct from the sciences, it must be, as we have said, because it is not a science at all, that is, it is not a pursuit of truth. Russell, according to Wittgenstein, is still guilty of confusion between science and philosophy in considering both of them as systems of true propositions.

There can be no philosophy as science if philosophy is an activity of clarifying meaning and sense, because, in order to arrive at the meanings of terms and the senses of propositions, we cannot go beyond the language activity and evaluate it by comparison with some external facts. When we explain the sense of a proposition by another proposition, this other proposition is taken to be understood or known directly and without any further explanation. And if that other proposition is itself not clear, then we must proceed with its clarification by some other proposition, and so on. But ultimately our clarification must stop. Clarification cannot be ultimately clarified: 'That which expresses *itself* in language, *we* cannot express by language' (*Tractatus,* 4.121). Thus, our clarification ultimately does not itself consist of propositions. Philosophy is not a system of propositions, is not a science.

Of course, Wittgenstein's definition of philosophy, like any definition, is arbitrary. The question may arise, however, whether this definition is in agreement with the accepted definitions of the term. To answer this matter-of-fact question, we would have to turn to historical investigation of the use of the term 'philosophy'. But if we do so, we find no unanimous agreement among the users of the term as to its precise meaning. We find it to be applied to the most diverse intellectual activities and accomplishments ranging from physics to metaphysics, and the only common feature we find in these may be expressed vaguely as a search for wisdom. On Wittgenstein's analysis this search for wisdom has two aspects generally confused in the history of philosophy: (a) the activity of creation and subsequent clarification of symbolism which is to serve as the medium of positive knowledge, in short, the pursuit of meaning and sense; and (b) the search for truth or positive knowledge of the world, expressed in propositions of our symbolism and verified by facts. These two aspects of the search for wisdom may be called philosophical and scientific, respectively. Traditional philosophy has often confused the two.

The pursuit of truth is the business of the activities of everyday life and of its refined extension, science. But before we can proceed to ascertain the truth or falsehood of a proposition, whether in science or in everyday life, we must understand what the proposition says: 'in order to be able to say "p" is true (or false) I must have determined under what conditions I call "p" true, and thereby I determine the sense of the proposition' (4.063). And it is the proper and the only business of philosophy to see to it that we understand the terms and propositions we use. Sometimes it happens that we proceed to verify a proposition without realizing that we are not clear as to what it says; we may not realize that we are using terms which have no clear meaning. Such things have happened even in scientific investigations, for example, in dealing with space and time. It is then the business of a philosopher in such situations to find out, or else to determine anew the precise meaning of the terms and the clear and unambiguous sense of the propositions used. When a scientist makes such a clarification of his language, he is acting in the capacity of a philosopher. Thus Einstein was engaged in philosophic activity when he offered a precise meaning to the term 'simultaneity'. And even in such a formal and nonfactual subject as mathematics much depends on clarifying linguistic confusions, such as the statement by Bernoulli that 'A quantity, which is increased or decreased infinitely little, is neither increased nor decreased'. Similar activity of clarification is needed in all walks of life, and a man of good common sense, when he is clarifying propositions and making precise terms in practical life, is a philosopher. Such, for example, was Socrates.

Whenever and wherever we face any problem, one of two things is possible: either (a) we understand the problem, or (b) we do not understand it. In the first situation there is no need of any philosophy, and the problem is to be solved by scientific methods. In the second situation we have to investigate the statement of the problem, and in doing this we can arrive at either of two results: (1) The problem after clarification becomes a genuine or real problem, and then we refer it for further investigation to science, and as a philosophical problem it simply disappears; or (2) it turns out to be no problem at all but a misunderstanding of our language, and it makes no sense at all to us.

Philosophers (even Russell) have not always seen clearly the distinction between the pursuit of meaning and sense on the one hand, and the pursuit of truth about the world on the other, and the confusion of the two has resulted in a great deal of nonsensical disputation and literature. This confusion very probably had its root in the historical fact that in ancient times philosophy was almost identical with the science of the times, because ancient science was in an embryonic stage, its concepts vague and ambiguous, and therefore the activity of scientists was almost subsidiary to the clarification of the meaning of these concepts, that is, to the philosophical activity. As the task of a scientist was primarily philosophical, it was only natural that the two activities were not clearly distinguished by the persons engaged almost constantly and simultaneously in both, especially as both tended to relieve the same feeling of intellectual discomfort. And this original confusion seems to have persisted more or less throughout the whole history of philosophy.

Traditional philosophy, after the special sciences had appropriated more and more of the various aspects and provinces of the world for their special attention, had misconceived its task to be the way of pursuing the truths inaccessible to science, the 'ultimate truths' beyond the sphere of science, and this misconception of its task invalidated a large part of the effort of traditional philosophers. Philosophy became the 'first' or fundamental science of the essential nature of things. Philosophers thought that, in addition to the special empirical truths of sciences and of everyday life, there are general or universal and more essential truths about the world to be attained by special philosophical, as contrasted to scientific, methods of (a) philosophical intuition, or (b) 'dialectical' or logical demonstration.

(a) The appeal to intuition in philosophy is usually due to one of the following two confusions: (1) confusion between cognition and immediate noncognitive experience, or (2) confusion between the psychological feeling of self-evidence on the part of the person stating a proposition, and the grounds of its truth or falsehood. (1) The first distinction, between cognition and immediate content, is very important in Wittgenstein's view, but not very clear to me, though I have dealt with it in discussing the form of propositions, and will return to it in my discussion of his mysticism. (2) The second kind of confusion hardly needs any discussion after it is pointed out, and it may be exemplified by the case of Mrs. John Mattern, the wife of the aviator. Mattern, when on his round-the-world solo flight in the summer of 1933, was lost and not heard from for a couple of weeks, and it was reasonably suspected that he was dead. But when the news came that he was alive and safe, Mrs. Mattern, in all seriousness, announced to the world that she had known this all along. The wish here happens to be, just as in the case of other 'intuitive' philosophers, the father not only of the thought but of the truth as well. 'The world', however, 'is independent of my will' (*Tractatus*, 6.373). (b) The belief in the possibility of arriving at a new truth about the world by logical demonstration is due to misunderstanding the nature of inference. Since all inference is tautological or analytical, no new significant propositions about the world can be obtained in that way: 'There is no picture which is a priori true' (2.225), and 'There is no order of things a priori' (5.634). Traditional philosophy by confusing philosophy with science became metaphysical and thus nonsensical. 'Certainly it was ordained as a scourge upon the pride of human wisdom, that the wisest of us should thus outwit ourselves, and eternally forego our purposes, in the intemperate act of pursuing them' (Sterne's *Tristram Shandy*).

And so, in addition to the task of clarifying the language of contemporary science and everyday life, contemporary philosophy has also what is essentially a negative task of analyzing the works of the great traditional philosophers, of sifting out scientific propositions found there from the properly philosophical work of clarification of language and weeding out the meaningless terms and nonsensical propositions. We must not dogmatically condemn as senseless all the work of the men who have been called philosophers. If a man pursues truth in the scientific way of observation of the world, then his work gives us real and important information about the world, even if the author has intermingled it with nonsensical speculations. Moreover, the works of great philosophers contain a great deal of the valuable philosophical work of clarification of language. But, on Wittgenstein's view, outside the properly philosophical activity of clarifying language, and the scientific activity of pursuing truth, there is no additional and special province for the philosophical pursuit of truth of a kind different from the truth accessible to science, and therefore we must reject as nonsense all the special 'philosophic problems' of traditional philosophy. The fate of all the special 'philosophic' problems, that is, problems about the world, not amenable to scientific treatment, is to disappear on a careful analysis of the statements expressing them:

Most propositions and questions, that have been written about philosophical matters, are not false, but senseless. We cannot, therefore, answer questions of this kind at all, but only state their senselessness. Most questions and propositions of the philosophers result from the fact that we do not understand the logic of our language. . . . And so it is not to be wondered at that the deepest problems are really *no* problems (4.003).

Kant held that there can be no solution to metaphysical problems, that is, problems concerned with the 'ultimate nature of things', because the things-in-themselves are not accessible to the methods of science. Wittgenstein goes farther and declares that all the problems which are in principle not solvable by the methods of science are simply nonsensical, and are due to a misuse of our language. An attempt to say something metaphysical, something that neither science nor common sense can say, is, according to Wittgenstein, but a solemn humbug made rather imposing in the history of philosophy by the special jargon of technical terminology.

As has been pointed out, the study of traditional philosophy may be valuable from Wittgenstein's point of view for two reasons: it may give us bits of information of scientific value, and it contains instructive examples of the clarification of language performed by great philosophers of the past. Another, rather curious, reason may be adduced from Wittgenstein's point of view for the study of traditional philosophy. Philosophy is, according to Wittgenstein, an activity of clarifying confusions of language. Now, the history of philosophy seems to show a widely spread human tendency to certain kinds of linguistic confusion, due perhaps to some vague but nevertheless deeply seated intellectual aberrations with which the reflective portion of mankind seems to be afflicted. Kant in his own way has noticed this ineradicable tendency as 'natural disposition', and has assigned to it a pragmatic or 'regulative' role within experience. The history of philosophy is largely the history of the intellectual pathology of reflective people who try to get out of their intellectual skins by means of some verbal contortions; it is the history of widely spread misuse of language. A study of the history of philosophy might serve, on this view of it, as a study of the special intellectual disorders to which reflective people are subject. This is the view of philosophy taken by Anatole France when he wrote: 'The philosophies are interesting solely as psychical monuments suitable to enlighten scholars on the various stages through which the human spirit has passed. Valuable for the study of man, they can give no information about anything that is not man' (*Garden of Epicurus*). Philosophy in Wittgenstein's sense—the activity of clarifying language—gets its pathos from what it destroys. It overthrows the false gods, and it is the importance ascribed to these false gods that gives importance to the activity of overthrowing them. Besides, during this process of destruction we may perhaps become aware in ourselves of the same intellectual tendencies which have caused even great minds to misuse language as they did; and, being conscious of these tendencies, we may, perchance, control them more or less effectively. 'Metaphysics', as C. S. Peirce once said—and we may extend this to all traditional philosophy, 'is a subject . . . the knowledge of which, like that of a sunken reef, serves chiefly to enable us to keep clear of it'.

A freshman discussing Descartes in an examination paper wrote, 'Descartes found that he was a being subject to ideas'. Perhaps the freshman is right, and the philosophy of Descartes was partly the consequence of this insidious malady, and partly the use of a psychoanalytic method of combating it. But all reflective people seem to be subject to the same malady, and, finding ourselves in such a hereditary predicament, we might as well make the best of it, and try to meet the danger as sensibly as we can. Study of philosophy may serve as a catharsis to the afflicted. The sensible thing seems to be to allow ourselves to indulge moderately in the study of the examples of this ineradicable affliction, in the hope that this homeopathic treatment will open a safe outlet to the same affliction in ourselves, just as wise teachers allow boys to play games and even fight with gloves in order to keep them out of mischief. Incidentally, herein lies the danger of supporting professional philosophers, a danger analogous to that of employing professional football coaches.

4.2   Among the important failings common to most traditional philosophers is, according to Wittgenstein, what may be called the fallacy of the angelic point of view. Perhaps this fallacy should be called 'the philosophers' fallacy'. It consists in the pretension of having avoided the logical restrictions of what is called in contemporary philosophical literature 'the egocentric predicament', that is, the pretension that one can say something about the world from a point of view which is outside the world in which one finds oneself. One tries to deal with the world from a point of view of another and fictitious world, of which our world is supposed to be but a proper part. A typical example of this fallacy is Descartes' pretension of starting with universal doubt. On Wittgenstein's analysis, this fallacy amounts to a linguistic confusion: one pretends to pass outside the limits of one's own language while still using it, to say what cannot be said, to think what cannot be thought. But, *'The limits of my language* mean the limits of my world. . . . What we cannot think, that we cannot think: we cannot therefore *say* what we cannot think' (5.6, 5.61). All the attempts to deal with the universe as a whole or with the 'ultimate' nature of things, that is, all metaphysics, are due to this fallacy of the angelic point of view.

This fallacy has been felt and recognized by traditional solipsism, as in that of Berkeley; but that solipsism itself fell victim to the very fallacy from which it was trying to escape; it became vicious or malicious solipsism: 'In fact what solipsism intends is quite correct, only it cannot be *said*, but it shows itself. That the world is *my* world, shows itself in the fact that the limits of the language (*the* language which only I understand) mean the limits of *my* world' (5.62). The correct idea ambiguously involved in solipsism is a tautology, but when intended as a significant factual proposition it involves a self-contradiction. This formal tautological nature of the notion of solipsism has been correctly spotted by Kant: 'This principle of necessary unity of apperception is itself, indeed, an identical, and therefore analytic proposition' (*Critique of Pure Reason*, B135). Traditional solipsism became vicious through its attempt to express itself as a significant factual proposition: it makes a statement of fact about the character of the world as a whole; and in order to do so it must take a point of view outside the world, i.e., an angelic point of view; it pretends to think both sides of the limit to its thinking. Traditional solipsism is very confused metaphysics.

As Wittgenstein insists, I can say nothing significant *about* my world as a whole because the distinction between my ego and the world cannot enter into my significant language: I cannot speak significantly of myself as an ego which is a part of my own world, and I cannot speak of any other world but mine: *'Where in* the world is a metaphysical subject to be noted? . . . The I in solipsism shrinks to an extensionless point and there remains the reality co-ordinated with it. . . . The I occurs in philosophy through the fact that "the world is my world". The philosophical I is not the man, not the human body or the human soul of which psychology treats, but the metaphysical subject, the limit—not a part of the world' (5.633, 5.64, 5.641). The 'metaphysical subject' of which Wittgenstein here speaks is not an entity but the formal limit of language. Wittgenstein's 'solipsism' is not factual but formal: it points to the impossibility of stating the limits of significant language by the propositions of such language itself. I feel that Wittgenstein here is very close to Kant, with the 'I' in his world playing the same role that 'Transcendental Unity of Apperception' plays in Kant's phenomenal world, namely, 'that unity of consciousness which precedes all data of intuitions, and by relation to which representation of objects is alone possible. This pure original unchangeable consciousness I shall name *transcendental apperception*. . . . The original and necessary consciousness of the identity of the self is thus at the same time a consciousness of an equally necessary unity of the synthesis of all appearance according to concepts, that is, according to rules' (*Critique of Pure Reason*, A107–08). Again, 'The abiding and unchanging "I" (pure apperception) forms the correlate of all our representations . . .' (*op. cit.*, A123).

Stated simply, the procedure of a naïve 'factual' solipsist is as follows. He starts with the world of common-sense realism, and considers his psychological self (whatever that may be) as only one part of this realistic world. Then he argues correctly, because tautologically, that his experience is all that he can experience. Next, he concludes incorrectly that, since the states of his psychological self are all that this self can experience, the rest of the original common-sense realistic world is either unreal or is but a part of what was originally thought to be its own part, namely, his psychological self. By shifting of meaning, the original psychological self now becomes a self-contained and closed entity, a Fichtean Ego, and the solipsist talks nonsense. The situation is vividly described by Tolstoi in his *Childhood, Boyhood and Youth*. Tolstoi recalls:

I imagined that besides me there are no existences in the world, that the objects are not objects, but are merely images which appear only when I direct my attention upon them, and that when I cease thinking about them, these images immediately disappear . . . what exists is not the objects but my relation to them. There were moments when under the influence of this fixed idea I was approaching to such a state of mental derangement that I hoped by quickly turning around to catch unawares the nothingness there where I was not.

This attempt 'to catch unawares the nothingness there where I was not' reveals the fundamental confusion of all naïve solipsism. The confusion is due, first, to the pretension of being able to observe one's own world from outside, from an angelic point of view; and, second, to the identification of this angelic self with a particular psychological self (in itself a very dubious entity).

Attempts by psychologizing epistemologists, such as Locke, to establish the limitation of human knowledge through the study of human faculties are all cases of vicious solipsism of varying degrees of complexity. They all tacitly presuppose that they can take the human mind, as the instrument of knowing, to be the object of their investigation, to be examined by them from outside itself, from some angelic point of view. Thus, starting theoretically from an outlook wider, by definition, than one possible to their own minds, they later on limit the region accessible to knowing by us to an island floating in this larger world not accessible to the human mind, and all through the discussion they assume themselves to be looking upon the world and their own minds in it from outside, from an angelic point of view. They tacitly assume right along the existence of this larger all-inclusive angelic world not to be known to their own minds, and then conclude tautologically that what their minds can know is not this real wider angelic world, but only their subjectively limited version of it. They are forever confined by the limitations of their own minds, as the instruments of knowing, within the narrow boundaries of human experience, but beyond these boundaries there *is*, it is assumed, a larger and all-inclusive world, but a world not knowable to their minds. In all seriousness they write volumes on what they themselves say (from an angelic point of view, of course) is entirely excluded from the range of their own minds. They assume that they can jump out of their intellectual skins and look at themselves as objects external to themselves, and then conclude and deplore the fact that the skin in which they actually live, after all, does not permit such jumping; all the while, nevertheless, assuming that they are, for the time of the discussion at least, outside their own skins; Wittgenstein simply points out that such intellectual equilibristics are logically impossible.

Theology is but a sort of supermetaphysics, and is due to the fallacy of the angelic point of view in even more exaggerated form than one resulting in metaphysics. While the metaphysician pretends to pull himself by his own ears into a position external to his world, a theologian claims a position from which he can discuss not only metaphysical reality beyond our experience, but the angelic position of the metaphysician itself. He pretends to be able to discuss not only the ultimate reality, but the creator of this reality as well. Theology says, of course, no more than metaphysics: both say nothing; it is nonsense squared, but (as zero squared in arithmetic still remains zero) it remains nonsense nonetheless: 'God does not reveal himself in the world' (*Tractatus,* 6.432) any more than angels do.

The essence of what is valid in solipsism cannot be stated by any significant proposition, but has to be grasped intuitively, because it is a formal and not a factual limitation upon our world. The 'truth' of solipsism is tautologous: we can discuss only the discussable, know only the knowable, and what we cannot say we simply cannot say, and we can't whistle it either, as F. P. Ramsey remarked. Any attempt to make a significant proposition out of these tautologies is an impossibility because it requires of us that we get entirely outside our language and then make a statement about our language while we are still using it: 'in order to draw a limit to thinking we should have to be able to think both sides of this limit (we should therefore have to be able to think what cannot be thought)' (*Tractatus,* Preface).

It must be added here that it is very important on Wittgenstein's view that when we say that a certain sentence in philosophy, or any sentence whatever for that matter, is senseless, we do not say that it is false. A senseless sentence can be neither true nor false. What we do intend to say on such occasions is that the sentence under consideration makes no sense for us, and that therefore we cannot pronounce on its truth or falsity. And in regard to metaphysics, Wittgenstein goes farther and says that, by the very nature of the undertaking, all metaphysical sentences are bound to be nonsensical. Materialism and idealism, if interpreted as metaphysics, are equally nonsensical. Materialism says, 'Everything is matter', idealism, 'Everything is mind'. If we interpret these statements to mean, respectively, 'Everything in our experience is describable by physics' and 'Everything in our experience is describable by psychology', the statements cease to be metaphysical and acquire sense. The question now becomes: What is the form of the laws of nature? And the problem now is scientific. Otherwise, the above statements are senseless. Even skepticism as a negative metaphysics is senseless: 'Scepticism is *not* irrefutable, but palpably senseless, if it would doubt where a question cannot be asked. For doubt can only exist where there is a question; a question only where there is an answer, and this only where something *can* be *said*' (6.51).

It must be also pointed out here that Wittgenstein's view does not raise any barrier to new experience and knowledge in the future. Concerning future propositions not yet formulated, we can make only formal restrictions: they will have to contain only terms which will have meaning in our experience, and will have to be so constructed as to make sense. As to the contents of what these meanings and senses will be we have absolutely nothing to say now. Wittgenstein does not deny that we shall be able to have entirely new experiences in the future; we can neither assert nor deny such experiences, any more than we can answer a letter which has not yet been written; entirely novel future experiences are like a clean slate to us now, and we cannot discuss them. To restrict future experiences in any but a formal way is to raise an unsurmountable and totally gratuitous obstacle to further inquiry, as would be the case with all metaphysics, if metaphysics made sense. Our present experience and the formal requirements of meaning and sense for future symbolism do not put any absolute limit or barrier to the possible future extension either of our experience or of the detailed symbolic formulations of our future knowledge.

Concerning propositions already formulated *now* about the future, two cases must be distinguished: (a) A proposition which may be so constructed as to make sense even if we are unable to decide upon the truth or falsity of the proposition. (b) A proposition which is really a pseudo-proposition, a sentence formed according to a certain grammatical order but which nevertheless makes no sense, a proposition the decision on the truth value of which is not merely difficult but impossible. A proposition about the geography of the other side of the moon in the year 2000 A.D. is an example of the first kind; a pseudo-proposition about the absolute size of the universe in the year 2000 A.D. is an example of the second. A proposition about the past or the future is legitimate if it makes sense to us now, even if we cannot in practice decide upon its truth value.

Thus, Wittgenstein puts no restrictions on the progress of experience and knowledge; he merely refuses to discuss what is, by definition, entirely disconnected from our present experience, and he rejects all futile attempts to answer senseless questions. By refusing to discuss anything outside of what is possible from our present point of view we merely refuse to talk nonsense, but we do not shut out any future experience or knowledge. And the only restrictions we can make upon our future knowledge are purely formal: our future terms must have meaning and our future propositions sense within the context of future experience, whatever that may be.

4.3   Before concluding my essay I wish to say a good word for Wittgenstein's mysticism. This aspect of Wittgenstein's view has been strongly depreciated if not outrightly condemned by Russell and Ramsey, the two persons otherwise most sympathetic toward Wittgenstein's view. But it seems to me that Wittgenstein's mysticism is definitely a very valuable and integral part of his view, and that it cannot be rejected without reducing the whole view to a narrow and dogmatic empiricism.

We must, I believe, admit that there are inexpressible aspects in our experience. To deny the inexpressibility of some aspects of our experience and thus their inaccessibility to communicable knowledge is equivalent to making the assertion that all and every experience is expressible and communicable, which is a case of a presumptuous and dogmatic rationalism. Wittgenstein used the adjective 'mystical' in the sense of 'inexpressible'. Of course, from the very nature of the situation it is a hopeless task to try to say anything informative about the mystical; but perhaps it may be possible to speak of it in a suggestive way. And, I hope, I will be able to show why I consider Wittgenstein's mysticism to be a very valuable part of his whole view.

We may approach Wittgenstein's view on mysticism by considering his view on knowledge. The term 'knowledge' is really ambiguous. We must distinguish knowledge proper from immediate awareness (see, for instance, Russell's *Problems of Philosophy,* pp. 72 f., 170 f.) These two are radically different kinds of knowledge, and we may distinguish the two, following Schlick, by the terms *cognition* and *intuition,* respectively. The fundamental difference between the two lies in the difference of logical structure of the two: cognition requires an apparatus of symbolism, while intuition cannot use any symbolism. In cognition we use some parts of our experience to represent certain other parts; cognition must include the two-termed relation of sign and signified; we cognize *by* means of signs interpreted according to the rules of our symbolism. Intuition is a direct and unsymbolic awareness of, or insight into, reality; in intuiting reality we do not divide it into signs and referends, but apprehend reality directly as Schopenhauer and Bergson say we do. For our purpose here the important consequence of this difference between the two kinds of knowledge is that cognition is expressible and communicable, while intuition is inexpressible and incommunicable.

What is grasped by intuition is a case of what Wittgenstein calls the *mystical:* 'There is indeed the inexpressible. This *shows* itself; it is the mystical' (6.522). Wittgenstein's mysticism is not metaphysical; it is not a theory about the world entirely outside our experience, as revealed by some special supernatural faculty. A theory is a set of propositions, requires language, is expressible. Mystic insight cannot be expressed by any propositions, and it does not give us truth. Truth is a correspondence of a proposition with facts, and can be a result only of cognition; the terms 'true' and 'false' do not apply to direct apprehension. Of course, I can talk about my direct apprehension after I experience it, but I cannot express in my talk the immediate content of that apprehension. At best I can say something significant of the condition under which I had the apprehension. Thus all that we can say about the world is a subject of cognition, but our experience is not exhausted by cognition:

We feel that even if *all possible* scientific questions be answered, the problems of life have still not been touched at all. Of course there is then no question left, and just this is the answer. The solution of the problem of life is seen in the vanishing of this problem. (Is not this the reason why men to whom after long doubting the sense of life became clear, could not then say wherein this sense consisted?) (6.52, 6.521).

It may be instructive here to contrast Wittgenstein with Bergson, the most illustrious contemporary philosopher advocating mysticism. Bergson is fundamentally right, but he fails by succumbing to the temptation of talking about what he himself considers to be inexpressible. Bergson's fallacy is to assign to intuition, or 'intellectual sympathy', a place within the naturalistic metaphysical scheme, by identifying intuition with instinct. He explains what he calls 'intellectual sympathy' in terms of a particular theory about the world, a kind of biological metaphysics. Bergson attempts, after all, to tell what reality is in itself, namely, the Life Force. All we can do, however, in this connection, is to point out the right attitude to be taken to apprehend reality, and not pretend to tell what reality is. We cannot express direct apprehension. Bergson rightly sees that discursive knowledge or cognition does not exhaust all our experience; but he is wrong in attempting to express the inexpressible, while depreciating cognition in its legitimate sphere. Bergson is not sufficiently Bergsonian. The true mystic must be silent: 'Whereof one cannot speak, thereof one must be silent' (*Tractatus, 7*).

Form, which I discussed in Chap. 2, is one of these mystical aspects of reality:

Propositions can represent the whole reality, but they cannot represent what they must have in common with reality in order to be able to represent it—the logical form. To be able to represent the logical form, we should have to be able to put ourselves with the propositions outside logic, that is outside the world. Propositions cannot represent the logical form: this mirrors itself in the propositions. That which mirrors itself in language, language cannot represent. . . . The propositions *show* the logical form of reality. They exhibit it (4.12, 4.121).

While it is by virtue of form that propositions represent reality, the form itself cannot in its turn be represented, but must be grasped intuitively. Form is mystical.

Let us take a fact p, and a proposition 'p_1' representing it; p and 'p_1', then, have a form in common. In understanding 'p_1' we grasp this form. Now, let us assume that we fail to understand 'p_1' and that 'p_2' is needed to explain it, because 'p_1' is in Chinese and we understand only English, and 'p_2' is in English. Then in understanding 'p_2' we grasp the form common to p, 'p_1', and 'p_2'. If we do not understand 'p_2', we have to have 'p_3', and so on, until we get to 'p_n', which we do understand. By understanding 'p_n' we mean a direct grasp of the form of its sense. The form of p, 'p_1', 'p_2', $\cdots$ has not vanished from 'p_n' but has reappeared there (elliptically, in ordinary languages). It survives or propagates itself through all the series from p to 'p_n', and cannot be gotten rid of without our losing the cognition of p altogether. But at the end of the series we still have to grasp this form directly, say from 'p_n', 'p_2', and so on, if we understood any of them, or from p itself, if we were directly confronted with it. The grasping of form in the ultimate instance is direct, by intuition. Hierarchy of languages suggested by Russell or, what amounts to the same thing, by Carnap's series of metalanguages would not eliminate the necessity of direct grasping of form: the last language of the hierarchical series still would have a form and that, according to Wittgenstein, would have to be apprehended directly. This is one of the points on which, according to Schlick, Wittgenstein was violently opposed to Carnap. Form can be present in any number of instances, and it is in virtue of this fact that it can serve as a means of communication. But experiencing of the form itself cannot be communicated; form must be grasped directly, intuitively: 'That which expresses *itself* in language, *we* cannot express by language' (4.121). Thus, while we can have cognition only because of the form, the form itself is not an object of cognition, but of intuition. It is mystical.

Another mystical aspect of reality is the immediate content of sense experience, for immediately experienced qualities— of color, sadness, duration, and so on. Take blue, for example. 'Blue' is a concept which has a meaning only within certain contexts. This meaning is due to the form of the circumstances under which blue may be experienced. In other words, the meaning of 'blue' is purely behavioristic. (There is a serious inconsistency in behaviorism here. Perhaps, following Schlick, we can avoid it by saying that what is known behavioristically is only the form and not the content of experience of several participants. I am not entirely convinced that the difficulty is really solved.) What Mr. N and I call 'blue' is due to the form of our behavior in certain circumstances, to the invariance of our responses to the variations of certain conditions in my world. But what I actually experience when confronted with a patch which Mr. N and I call 'blue', and what is confined to my unique experience at the time, is the content. This content, we notice, is not, in contrast to the form, repeatable.

The disconcerting view of Wittgenstein—that one is limited in direct experience of qualities to the contents of what only he himself experiences, seems to imply that I am precluded from any intimate relations with other people, and must confine myself to purely behavioristic relationships—a truly distressing situation: '. . . if there were not some community of feeling among mankind, however varying in different persons—I mean to say, if every man's feelings were peculiar to himself and were not shared by the rest of his species—I do not see how we could ever communicate our impressions to one another' (Plato's *Gorgias*, 481C). But, very fortunately, this terrible conclusion does not necessarily follow, even if we accept Wittgenstein's mysticism. Though we cannot experience the very same sense contents, we may yet participate in the same values, for values, we notice, are outside the world and, perhaps, can be grasped by the mystic intuition of any number of persons, just as form can: 'If there is a value . . . it must lie outside all happening and being-so. . . . It must lie outside the world . . . there can be no ethical propositions. . . . Ethics are transcendental' (6.41, 6.42, 6.421). And, according to Wittgenstein, we can intuit this transcendental inexpressible region; intuition of it is the mystical feeling: 'The solution of the riddle of life . . . lies *outside* space and time' (6.4312); 'men to whom after long doubting the sense of life became clear, could not then say wherein this sense consisted. There is, indeed the inexpressible. . . ; it is the mystical' (6.521, 6.522).

Finally, and here personally I emphatically agree with Wittgenstein—the world as a whole is also mystical: 'Not *how* the world is, is the mystical, but *that* it is. The contemplation of the world sub specie aeterni is its contemplation as a limited whole. The feeling of the world as a limited whole is the mystical feeling' (6.44, 6.45). Here we are back again to the rejected angelic point of view, but with a difference. Now we can take it, not cognitively, only intuitively; and this imposes upon us an important restriction: we cannot say anything when we take that vantage point of view. We can have no symbol which is a part of the world and which yet can represent this whole world as an object of cognition. A map of the whole world (a case of Royce's map on a cosmic scale) is impossible, because the reflexive relation needed to accomplish this purpose is a self-contradictory notion, just as a round square is. But our contemplation of the world as a whole is not a cognitive process through language, but an intuitive and direct grasp which lies outside the pale of discourse. The detailed study of the world, of the *how* of the world, is the business of science. The ultimate grasp of the world as a whole can be accomplished only through the mystic insight. 'Philosophy', said Plato, 'begins in wonder'; and—I should like to add—in the last count it ends in wonder, too.

These few examples of the mystical will show, I hope, why I think that mysticism is an important part of Wittgenstein's view. Mysticism becomes the last refuge for the most cherished things in life, in fact for all values, for all that cannot be discussed and yet is of the utmost importance to us. As C. S. Peirce remarked, 'On vitally important topics reasoning is out of place . . . all sensible talk about vital topics must be commonplace, all reasoning about them unsound, and all study of them narrow and sordid' (*Collected Papers,* Vol. I, 1.652, 1.677). In his denial of the cognitive knowledge of the sense of life, Wittgenstein, after all, is essentially in agreement with many other philosophers.

4.4 And so we conclude that as philosophers we have nothing significant to say, that is, no factual information to convey: what can be significantly said can be said by the propositions of everyday life or its refined extension, science; and what in principle cannot be said by science is either nonsense or belongs to the realm of the mystical, but in either case cannot be expressed by language.

Philosophy for Wittgenstein is not a doctrine about the world, but an activity of clarifying our language; and instead of answering questions it aims, as Ramsey puts it, at curing headaches. We are impelled to philosophize by the feeling of intellectual discomfort which we experience whenever our language is not clear and unambiguous, and the philosophical task terminates as soon as the linguistic confusion we meet with is eliminated. This function of a philosopher is but a modernized version of the view expressed in a passage in Plato:

They cross-examine a man's words, when he thinks he is saying something and is really saying nothing, and easily convict him of inconsistencies in his opinions. . . . He, seeing this, is angry with himself, and grows gentle towards others, and thus is entirely delivered from great prejudices and harsh notions, in a way which is most amusing to the hearer, and produces the most lasting good effect on the person who is the subject of the operation . . . he must be purged of his prejudices first and made to think that he knows only what he knows, and no more (*Sophist,* 230).

Wittgenstein's main purpose in the *Tractatus* was to make the reader realize this point. The *Tractatus* was not intended to teach anything factual to anybody. What Wittgenstein tries to convey can be grasped directly by those who will take the right attitude consequent on reading the *Tractatus;* and that attitude cannot be given in the *Tractatus,* but may only be stimulated by reading it: 'My propositions are elucidatory in this way: he who understands me finally recognizes them as senseless, when he has climbed out through them, on them, over them. (He must so to speak throw away the ladder, after he has climbed up on it). He must surmount these propositions; then he sees the world rightly' (6.54).

But while pointing out the tautological limitation of knowledge to the knowable, the *Tractatus* has also brought out the immensely important positive insight: the knowable does not exhaust reality, and there are things in life which cannot be discussed. But concerning these we cannot speak, and 'Whereof one cannot speak, thereof one must be silent' (7).

A quotation from Plato's *Theaetetus* might have served as a fitting conclusion to the *Tractatus,* and at the same time perhaps as an expression of the hope of its author: 'If, Theaetetus, you should ever conceive afresh, you will be all the better for the present investigation, and if not, you will be soberer and humbler and gentler to other men, and will be too modest to fancy that you know what you do not know. These are the limits of my art; I can no further go . . .'.